West Virginia Dogman

by Dave Spinks

Editor

Linda Harkcom

Foreword

Ken Gerhard

Contributors

Dr. Raymond Keller
Joedy Cook

Art

Ron Lanham
Jamie Snell - Rougarou

Published in the United States of America by
Starborn Illumination Publishing
P.O. Box 666
Mt.Pleasant, PA 15666
www.si-pub.com

TABLE OF CONTENTS

EVEN A MAN WHO IS PURE OF HEART

AND SAYS HIS PRAYERS BY NIGHT

MAY BECOME A WOLF

WHEN THE WOLFBANE BLOOMS

AND THE AUTUM MOON IS BRIGHT

Curt Siodmak

Foreword

By
Ken Gerhard

Longtime students of cryptozoology are intimately familiar with all the major players – Bigfoot, Nessie, Jersey Devil, Mothman, Chupacabra, et al. However, there has been a newcomer on the scene as of late, whose meteoric rise in popularity cannot be ignored.

Generally characterized as displaying a powerful, manlike torso and arms, with two slightly bowed legs, oddly topped with a wolf-like head, the startling creature has been spotted lurking near the fringe of dark forests everywhere since the early 1990s. Evidently originating in the American Midwest, (specifically Wisconsin and Michigan), the apparition called "Dogman" has now been reported on virtually every continent.

Television programs, as well as immensely trendy podcasts where eyewitnesses call in and describe their encounters in frightening detail, have contributed to the monster's aspiring acclaim. Yet, from a zoological perspective, there are colossal issues. Unlike the Sasquatch, sea monsters, thunderbirds, black panthers and other traditional cryptids, Dogman belongs in an enigmatic category along with other improbable man-beasts such as flying humanoids, mermaids and the so-called "Goatman." There is simply no indication in the fossil record that such things could exist. Canids and Homo sapiens last shared a common ancestor some 66 million years ago, around the time that dinosaurs went extinct. There is simply no evidence that these distinct lineages, which evolved in dramatically different directions, would ever converge again.

Introduction

Even before Christ, werewolves have instilled a sense of primordial fear in humans. The wolf in general is one of the most dangerous, and most cunning, of all the natural predators known to man. They hunt in packs and each pack has an Alpha male, or in some cases a female, that has been chosen by the rest of the pack as being the fittest to be the leader of that pack. If you combine these characteristics with human traits, along with the supernatural blood lusting aspect of a werewolf, this being becomes a formidable force to deal with.

These creatures live in the shadows and implore a stealthy stalking mechanism to hunt down and kill their victims. Werewolves have a long association with other nefarious beings such as vampires, witches, and demons. There is an even closer association with black dogs and dogmen. For centuries, numerous cases have been documented concerning marauding werewolves going on killing sprees, killing both man and beast alike. These reports instilled so much fear in local villages around the world that normal wolves were hunted into extinction in some areas and extremely near to extinction in others. In modern times, we rarely hear of rampaging wolves or reports of werewolves going on killing sprees. But make no mistake, although cases and reports are a rarity in today's times, there are still some that arise from time to time. These reports usually come out of rural areas of the world, such as West Virginia, where the Folklore is still alive and thriving to this day.

To better understand what the werewolf or dogman is, we must examine the characteristics and history of where these creatures stem from and how are they created. By definition, a werewolf is a human who transforms into a wolf and later resumes back to human form. There are several variations of this transformation, but all are similar in nature.

First recorded in the 11th century, these creatures have always had close associations with evil or demonic forces. The word "werewolf," was recorded in the ordinances of King Cnut" (1017-1037), as another word for the devil.

Another name for werewolves is "lycanthropes." This stems from the Greek term for "man-wolf," which came from the name of King Lycaon of Greek Mythology. It is said that the King was turned into a wolf as a method of punishment for consuming human flesh by the God Jupiter.

Still yet another name for this creature is a Skinwalker. This term has been long feared by many Native American tribes in the United States, so much so that even speaking this word or saying it in each tribe's native tongue is considered very taboo. It is thought to bring about bad omens upon you, and your tribe.

For centuries reports of werewolves and dogmen were told all over Ireland, England, Italy, and Germany. Many of these tales talk about how these creatures would stalk and kill villagers. In most cases, large hunting parties would gather to hunt, track down and kill the beasts. Some accounts claim that silver was the only thing that could kill these supernatural creatures. In some reports, once the beast was shot or run through with a silver bullet or blade, the beast would then return to its human form. However, these types of accounts seem to be more of Hollywood's perception on how to take down one of these monsters.

It makes sense that with the mass immigration to America by so many Europeans over the centuries, that they would bring their folklore, history, and personal accounts to the new world. In fact, if any immigrants from those counties rich in werewolf lore were, somehow, bewitched or infected with these so-called werewolf genes or curses, their ancestors may be living among us today, infecting others and carrying on their legacies. It would also make sense that the Native American tribes of North America would not have stopped their practices and beliefs of skinwalkers or other similar supernatural wolf like beings walking among us.

X

West Virginia is rich in Native American traditions as well as those of the Irish, German, and Italian due to the number of immigrants from those countries over the centuries. When it comes to dogmen, werewolves, and black dog sightings and encounters, one thing is for certain, there are historical accounts. There are even regularly reported modern sightings here in the mountain state.

Chapter I

History of the Werewolf

Although it is not known for sure how, when and where the legends of the werewolf began, what is known is that these nightmarish creatures seemed to have made their first appearance in "The Epic of Gilgamesh." According to the poem, Gilgamesh rejected a woman who wanted to be his lover because during a fit of rage, she turned a previous mate into a wolf.

In today's world, most people have heard of werewolves, but few know of the ancient race of dog-headed men, better known as the Cynocephali. This creature is essentially a man with the head of a dog and the body of a man. They were known as a violent and very aggressive race, that could understand language but could not speak, only for making grunts and bark sounds much like regular dogs.

There are several reasons why these creatures were thought to have once existed here on earth in relatively large numbers. Reports from famous explorers such as Marco Polo and Christopher Columbus described them in detail.

In 400 B.C. A Greek named Ctesias described the Cynocephalus tribes as having no language but barked like dogs. Their teeth are much larger than normal dogs and their claws similar but much longer and rounder than normal dogs. He said they inhabited in the mountains as far as the river Indus, which originates in Tibet and runs southward through the Himalayas.

They can understand the local languages, but can only communicate with hand gestures as a reply. They eat raw meat and number in the 120,000 range. Furthermore, they survive by hunting and can trade with the king of India, whom in return sends them numerous weapons every five years.

They are very aggressive and cannot be defeated in battle due to the rough mountainous regions they reside in that are nearly inaccessible to humans. They live in caves, are very fast on foot. Both men and women have tails above their hips, like dogs, but theirs is longer and bushier than normal dogs. They have a much greater life span than humans, and some live up to 200 years. It is said that they were a very cruel race and would eat anyone they could if the opportunity presented itself.

The most famous Cynocephalus is Christianity's Saint Christopher, who was described in several texts as having the body of a man but the head of a dog. Originally, the future saint was said to have been a wild and fierce warrior who was captured in battle in Cyrenaica. Not only was this creature a very large man with a dog's head, but came from a warrior tribe of dog-headed men who looked like him. According to Christian mythology, he eventually met Jesus Christ and learned the error of his former ways. He repented, became baptized, and eventually received sainthood along with the gift of a human appearance. Multiple historical images show Saint Christopher as having the head of a dog.

No one knows for sure what happened to this small, but powerful race. Perhaps they were, in fact, a race of extraterrestrials, as is talked about later in this book. But one thing is most certain, they were a warring race who would have preferred death in battle rather than becoming subservient to another race's cultures and beliefs.

One can't help but wonder if this ancient race of dog-headed humanoids is related to the various types of semi-wolf, semi-human creatures such as the werewolf. When considering the history of werewolves, this sparsely

Saint Christopher

known race of beings may just prove to be a missing link in the mystery of their existence.

Another early example of werewolf tales being reported throughout history, is the legend of Lycaon, son of Pelasgus. The story says that the almighty Zeus became enraged at Lycaon for feeding him a meal that consisted of the remains of a sacrificed boy. Zeus punished Lycaon for his sins by turning him and his sons into werewolves.

Saint Christopher

Early in Nordic Lore, there is a story about a man and his son who happened upon mysterious wolf pelts. These pelts were said to have had the power to transform people into wolves while wearing them for ten days. Not long after the pair discovered the pelts, they decided to wear them and were transformed into rampaging wolves who went on a killing spree in the forest. The only thing that stopped the bloodthirsty madness was the father turned on his son, causing a wound that would be fatal. However, the untimely death of the boy would be stopped due to raven appearing on the scene and giving the father a leaf that had miraculous healing powers.

In North America, many Native American tribes have passed down history orally for thousands of years, and many of these tribes tell of a creature known as a Skinwalker. These creatures are kin to some sort of evil witch doctor. The witch doctor made a deal with evil forces by killing a member of their tribe or even a close family member to gain powers. These powers allowed them to take the form of any animal or even people, including a werewolf type creature.

In the Fifteenth century, a man by the name of Peter Stubbe was considered by many to be the most notorious werewolf of all. According to the stories, he transformed into a werewolf type creature at night and consumed many people in the city of Bedburg, Germany. Being blamed for these gory killings, he was soon cornered by a group of hunters sent to find him. Once the hunters got to him, they claimed that they witnessed Peter shape-shift from the form of a wolf back into a human. Under savage tortures, Peter confessed to the killings, and he too suffered a brutal execution. But before he could be executed, he claimed to have a magic belt that allowed him to change into a wolf at will. He admitted to killing women, kids, as well as men and eating their flesh. His magic belt was never found, and it is thought by some that he was the victim of a political witch-hunt. Nevertheless, his story and execution sparked fear of werewolves for generations near his home place.

There are many other fascinating and disturbing stories from all over the world of people who were essentially mass killers, who either claimed to be a werewolf or have a Magical artifact or substance that could turn them into one. France was no exception. In the early 1500s, Michel Verdun and Pierre Burgot were said to have become disciples of Satan. The pair claimed they possessed an ointment that would turn them into wolves. The two were responsible for the murders of several children. Once the two murderers were apprehended, they were burned alive at the stake.

Another well-known werewolf story from France was that of Giles Ganier who was affectionately dubbed the "Werewolf of Dole." According to the accounts, while in wolfman form, he would savagely kill children and eat them. Like his counterparts, he too suffered the grim fate of being burned alive at the stake.

As for those affected by these horrific attacks upon their kin folk and friends, one thing is certain, to them, a normal human being surely could not be responsible for these horrific acts of cannibalism and killings. To them, it had to be a real-life flesh and blood creature known as the werewolf.

For eons, people have blamed unknown beasts for acts that were simply too horrible in nature to explain rationally. In many cases, it could have been wolves that did, in fact, kill and eat people or in other cases, even bears. But one still must wonder about the cases where numerous eyewitnesses saw a man transform into a dogman or wolfman type creature or vice versa from a wolflike creature back into man. Surely mass hallucination is not always the case when it comes to some reports.

Common Indo-European lore shows the wolf was widespread throughout the Indo-European territory. It also indicates its cultic and ritual significance, which is clearly attested in the oldest Indo-European traditions.

The early European and Indo words for wolf, Gamkrelidze and Ivanov have been well documented in murals from a site in Turkey which has been dated at roughly 7000 years old.

Farther back in time, 11,000 BCE, early cave drawings and Mesolithic images of wolves and men hunting together have been found. An even earlier image of a wolf can be found in a cave in the Dordogne region of France. These images date to approximately 15,000 BCE.

Early warrior bands were widespread and deep-rooted in werewolf lore. They were initiated into these brotherhoods by wearing wolf pelts, masks, and cloaks. Over many years, they played roles in the sacrifices that coincided with the winter solstice.

In Gaulish mysticism, the word for werewolf is reconstructed from the words donios, meaning human, and uailos, meaning howler. In many cultures, such as the Gauls, it is believed that if you speak a monster's name, you may inadvertently call it into existence. Since it is taboo, the word howler is used, in place of the monster's name, to prevent this from happening.

In many areas of Europe including Spain, France, Germany, England, Ireland and more, there was a widespread belief that every soul that was infected under the curse of a werewolf, was doomed to return as a vampire.

In one grave, archaeologists found remains that showed evidence of torture prior to death, including significant damage to the chest cavity suggesting a stake through the heart. The person had also been beheaded, and partially dismembered before burial. All graves in the cemetery faced east in the direction of the rising sun except for this grave, which faces west. The severed

"The Werewolf or the Cannibal"
Lucas Cranach the Elder, 1592

head of the woman had also been placed unusually, with the back of her head toward her neck.

During that time, it was believed that a dead werewolf would surely become a vampire. Therefore, the victims of that werewolf would turn into a werewolf or vampire of the same curse.

In Russia, beliefs in a human being possessed by evil spirits have been known since the Middle Ages. In some more rural areas, these beliefs still survive today. This includes in the belief that animal spirits can and do possess humans.

The wolf is the national animal of the Chechen nation. The symbolic and metaphorical associations of the wolf stretch deep into Chechen history, with many positive idiomatic uses of wolf. According to Chechen mythology, God had created sheep for the wolf to enjoy, but man tricked it out of its 'patrimony', so it had to resort to ruse and robbery to reclaim its right. The cult of the wolf was widespread in olden times. These peoples held the belief that the tail and tendons of wolves held magical properties. Wolf teeth and bones, crafted into amulets, were hung around the necks of children as a protection from disease, malevolent spirits, and evil eyes.

In Livonia, an 80-year-old man, named Theiss, was tried for heresy in the 17th century. He claimed to be a member of a cult of werewolves who were charged with fighting the devil. The judges did not like his defense, and he was banished after being flogged severely. A historian named Carlo Ginzberg chronicled the event in a paper and suggested this man was a part of the agrarian Benandanti cult of werewolves from Northern Italy. He went on to say that this was direct evidence of an ancient shamanic shape-shifting cult.

In today's world, humans as a species are much more educated when it comes to knowing the animals that inhabit this planet. Then again, new species of animals that were previously unknown to the scientific community are being discovered quite regularly. We as humans are most definitely fallible and are constantly learning and evolving. We must not ever underestimate the possibility of the supernatural nor metaphysical side of the unexplained when it comes to dogmen.

Most people feel that these creatures are merely dreamed up monsters from Hollywood, such as the infamous movie "The Wolf Man" from 1941 that spawned countless other movies concerning the werewolf phenomena. Make no mistake, Hollywood of course elaborates, exaggerates, and even makes up these types of things. But I can assure you, at least some part of these stories stems from actual historical accounts and encounters that date back hundreds, if not thousands of years.

One thing is for sure, the legends of these dogmen and or werewolves will most certainly be carried on in West Virginia and around the world.

Chapter II

Dogmen/Werewolf Characteristics

One thing is consistent when it comes to tales of the Dogman, most stories describe a complete change in consciousness. They say that when in "wolf" form, the person is completely out of control of their "human" senses and moralities, causing them to give in to bloodlust and instinct. Usually, the stories of werewolves involve confusion, guilt, and regret when the "wolf" turns back to their human form.

Among the earliest accounts of the werewolf phenomenon are those reported by Petronius and Gervais of Tilbury. According to lore, werewolves can be created from a bite received from another werewolf or a wolf infected with a werewolf type of virus. In the creation story of this beast, lore suggests the symbolic power of moon cycles.

Such importance of cycles is reinforced by another facet of werewolf lore, that being the transformation from human to werewolf on the full Moon. Werewolf myths were found throughout Europe prior to the Middle Ages. Yet, it was also believed that later Christian norms and values provided an even more dramatic filter through which the werewolf was cast as the potential dark side or sinful nature that lies dormant within humans. Whereas before this, it is likely the tales were more heavily influenced by the average person's fear of living in villages susceptible to rampaging wolf packs or the occasional lone wolf.

Earlier pre-Christian accounts of werewolf stories also have to do with the belief in communing with various animals. They were less about one who was "cursed" to turn into a werewolf and more about the ability to work with the power of the wolf as a personal totem.

Werewolf symbolism is associated with the idea of being cursed or afflicted with an ailment or condition that recurs on a cyclical basis. Some have speculated whether accounts of werewolf phenomenon were really circumstances in which ailments of the body or mind gave way to extreme changes in mood or appearance.

Exploring the werewolf myth from a psychological standpoint, we can see the symbolism as related to fear of being overtaken by repressed or subconscious emotions. This is even more striking when you consider the link between the moon and the subconscious mind.

The Moon is a body associated with emotions, the subconscious, and intuition. The Moon has the power to signal our instinctive and primal urges, and this is also part of the symbolism of werewolf. The werewolf is our primal, wild inner self and our connection to instinct and raw power, which can also mean raw emotional energy and destructive instincts.

Just as the werewolf story involves a release of raw emotion often followed with a cyclical return to rationality and subsequent period of guilt or remorse, it symbolizes the lessons about the importance to express emotion with care and moderation. If there is nothing balancing the expression of wild inner rage or desire, then we can end up in regrettable situations.

According to lore, the only way to destroy a werewolf is with a silver bullet. Silver is also correlated to the Moon in esoteric and occult lore; thus, the Moon not only brings the beast out of the man, but also can subdue the primal urges.

The werewolf archetype in Tarot can be associated with the Moon card as this card connotes cycles and phases and of course for the obvious connection between the werewolf and the Moon. The Moon card is also about subconscious desires and fears. The Temperance card can also correspond to the werewolf, as temperance and moderation are the antidote to the extremes and emotional tides embodied by the werewolf.

In astrology, the werewolf corresponds to the Moon and the sign of Cancer, as this is the sign ruled by the movements of the Moon. When a werewolf is triggered by the Moon's cycle, the symbolism is akin to deep emotions caused by the influence of the Moon on our intuition and subconscious mind.

If you find the werewolf Spirit Animal is collaborating with you, you may feel as if your resolve is being tested. Some signs the werewolf Spirit Animal is working with you include, if deeply suppressed emotions are suddenly surging to the surface, or you are feeling pulled in new directions by instincts and intuition that you do not fully understand. Also, if you feel like you are on the verge of losing control of your calm, intellectual side, the werewolf Spirit Animal may be influencing you.

When a werewolf Spirit Animal is guiding you, remember the goal is always integration. There is no need to sacrifice the proverbial "wolf" to save the human side of your nature. The werewolf Spirit Animal's primal howl may be calling you back to your roots to help you heal emotions and prepare for a cycle in which you need to express your power in new ways.

If the werewolf arrives in your dreams, it can be an indication that you are feeling out of control. Your subconscious mind may be expressing that you are trying too hard to stifle some deeper emotions, or that you fear what will happen if you lose control of your emotional side.

Werewolf dreams may also signal the beginning of a new growth cycle or a cycle of personal transformation. You may feel as if you are dredging up

messy and unflattering emotions before you get the chance to establish a new foundation. The werewolf may be encouraging you to face, accept and integrate the creative and emotional sides of your nature.

According to Linda S. Godfrey's book, "Real Wolfmen–True Encounters in Modern America," wolfmen or dogmen are like a werewolf in some respects, but very characteristically different in other ways. These creatures do not appear to be humans, who experience a monthly transformation with the phases of the moon. Rather, they are in a class of creatures all by themselves. As noted by Godfrey, wolfmen are prevalent in heavily wooded areas, areas near water, and locations of Native American significance, particularly near burial mounds.

In some legends, werewolves can shape-shift at will due to a curse placed upon them. Others say that the person must have in their possession some sort of magical device, such as a cloak made from an enchanted wolf pelt or a magic potion. Still yet others claim people were turned into a werewolf after being bitten or scratched by another werewolf.

In many werewolf accounts, a person who is a werewolf can only turn into the creature when there is a full Moon. Most feel that is purely a Hollywood ideation. However, there may be more to that theory than most even realize.

There have been many studies conducted around the world that concluded that a full Moon literally brings out the beast in many humans. In one hospital in Australia, there was a study of a year-long period where more than 90 violent incidents occurred there during that time frame. The researchers discovered that over 20% of these incidents happened during a full Moon. While those incidents took place, the patients displayed bizarre behaviors such as spitting, scratching, and biting staff members.

Chapter III

Native American Lor

Native Americans have incredibly profound and fascinating beliefs, many of them involving wolves. To several tribes (past and present), the wolf itself is known as a protective spirit or totem. They view the wolf as a wise fellow hunter to be respected and admired.

Despite what many people may think, Hollywood was not the one that came up with the Native American belief in werewolves. It's a fact that this is a very old belief among many tribes. Since Hollywood is causing a stir of interest in Native American lore and beliefs, we will shed some light on the subject.

Many Tribes talk of men or even women possessing the power to transform from man to beast. In many tribes, including the Mohawk which once inhabited upstate New York and into Quebec, those that could shift were called limmikin and at times yenaloosi.

Skinwalkers

The Navajo Tribe is best known for its shape-shifter traditions and lore. They are called Skinwalkers by the Navajo or yeenadlooshi in their native tongue, which means "he goes on all fours." According to Navajo tradition, Skinwalkers will even look physically different from normal people – the main difference being their eyes, which are large and glowing, even in day-light. It is thought that if someone looks a Skinwalker in the eyes, they can absorb a person and "steal their skin." It is understood that someone should avoid looking for anyone suspected of being a Skinwalker and if you do suspect someone may be one, you never look at them with eye-to-eye contact. They are also believed to have no genitals and their skin is rock hard, making it impervious to axes and arrows.

In some versions of the tradition, the Skinwalker's tongue would be black, proof that their soul was poison. It is believed that becoming a Skinwalker is caused by dark forces. A person who becomes one of these evil beasts is believed to have done something immoral to attract that darkness. Furthermore, a Skinwalker does not take just one form, the creature can take many forms, such as owls, crows, coyotes, but one of the most common forms was wolf. While in animal form they lost all trace of humanity, the beast and animal instincts took over, making them vicious and unpredictable. This was only one version though; another is that while in animal form they were much more intelligent. They were also able to read minds and could lure people out of their homes and into the woods by imitating the voices and cries of loved ones.

It is thought that Skinwalkers are a type of witch that garners their superhuman powers by killing a nearby relative. This, in its plainest form, it is no different from performing a sacrifice as a tradeoff for magical powers. After performing this ritual these Skinwalkers would then be able to take the form of a creature based on their personal preference, however, they most ordinarily show up as wolves, owls, coyote's, foxes, and crows. These witches are known to be amazingly risky, and you would prefer not to experience one for dread of summoning their fierceness. These Skinwalkers can normally be discovered stalking victims in the southwest desert, although there have been reports of such creatures all over the east coast as well.

Skinwalker Ranch, which is in Utah, has been home to some weird things. Native Americans in the area genuinely believe that the area is cursed by

Skinwalker

evil spirits. The farm became infamous when the Sherman family came out to the media about their encounters living in that area. Their accounts included bizarre lights, spooky phantoms, and the story of an invulnerable wolf. The Sherman family came across a nice wolf, so nice it moved toward them. Tragically, however, the wolf slaughtered some of their steers, which are costly to come by. This provoked the leader of the Sherman family to shoot it with a magnum, and when he did, nothing happened. The wolf was shot repeatedly, yet the creature was not fazed. Feeling more determined, Sherman shot the wolf a few additional times, and it simply walked away. Was this an actual experience with a Skinwalker? Who knows?

In West Virginia, there are tales about creatures that are remarkably similar in description to a Skinwalker. They are said to stalk anyone who trespasses on sacred Native American lands. In the Mountain State, it is known that if you violate these sacred areas in any way, that you may find yourself a victim of one of these monsters.

Then there are the Hopi Indian traditions, where shapeshifting is brought on by a special ceremony known as Ya-Ya. The details of this ceremony are extremely secret and well-protected, but it is thought to involve wearing the skin of the animal one wishes to become.

Cherokee Traditions

The Cherokee were one of the so-called "Five Civilized Tribes". Known for their cultural wealth, language, and traditions. They are undoubtedly one of the native cultures that has had the greatest impact on Western society. We know of their stories, rituals, and their mysticism. They were transcribed in interesting books such as Cherokee Clans by Professor Panther-Yates.

In Cherokee lore, the sudden appearance of a white wolf heralds a magic, premature death. Over time, the white wolf became a white dog in Appalachian lore. The dog is large and powerful in build, a handsome creature despite hair that is matted and unkept. The dog shows up on roads, follows people home, and sits at a distance from dwellings as though waiting for someone. The white dog does indeed wait-not for a friend or a lost owner, but for a death. It is seen by the person who is about to die, and sometimes by others who are close to the person. The dog is invisible to others. Once the white dog appears, the person is marked for death and dies tragically within a few days or two weeks.

As part of their immense legacy, the Cherokee legend of the two wolves is one of the most popular. The story of the two wolves tells of a continuous battle between two forces inside

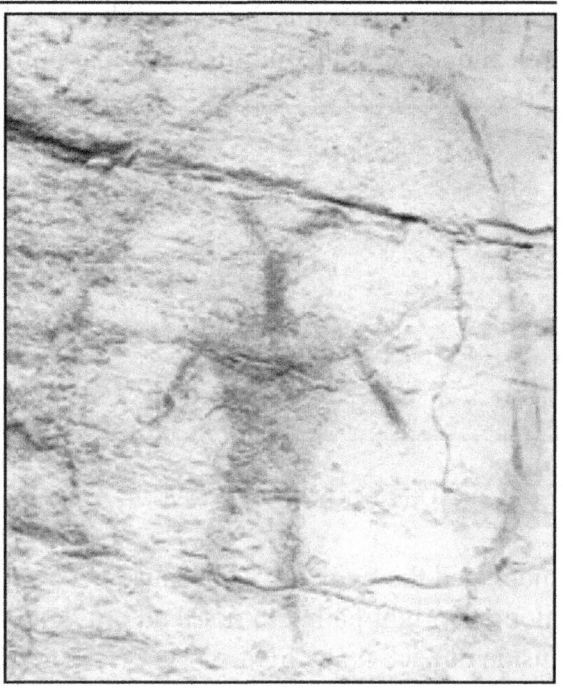

Native American cave art of werwolf.

us. It is a conflict between our darker side (the black wolf) with our more luminous and noble side (the white wolf). That duality that is in all of us between good and evil, joy and pride, guilt and humility, that defines much of who we are. You've heard this story before. While there is some doubt about whether this is really a Cherokee legend, there are certain references included in the oral tradition of small social groups of the Southern Appalachians.

The story is told as a wise lesson from an old man to his grandson. He explains that a terrible battle between two wolves takes place every day inside the hearts of all men.

These two animals symbolize two opposing forces. One is evil, the old man tells his grandson. It is anger. It is envy, greed, arrogance and even sadness.

It is the feeling of inferiority and the ego. The other force is kindness, joy, love, hope, serenity, humility, compassion, and of course, peace.

Cave painting of werwolves.

When the young Cherokee asked his grandfather which wolf is going to win that battle, in most versions, he responds: the one you choose to feed will win. But there is another version, much more interesting as well.

It is a tale about the old Cherokee warrior telling his grandson that both must win. Because the battle is not a matter of strength, but of balance. We must feed the two wolves because we need both. We must guide them both along the right path. Do not feed only one wolf: they must both be present inside of each man.

There are moments in our life when we feel like we are on a roller coaster. Everything is up and down. There are moments when we enjoy immeasurable joy, and moments when without knowing why, adversity, sadness, anger, and despair comes down on us.

Life can be happy or sad, benevolent, or brutal. Humans weave complex stories of love and hate, of serenity and loss. We are aware that, effectively, inside us there are always two opposing forces that we are not completely able to control. They fight fierce battles inside us.

This Cherokee legend of the two wolves explains that it is not about feeding a lone wolf and starving the other. People are a stable mix of a yin and a yang. It is a duality where, far from discarding or hiding a part of us, we must take it into account, make it visible and control it to live in balance.

The old warrior tells his grandson that if he chooses to only feed the white wolf, the black wolf will hide in every corner and stalk him whenever he sees him weak or off guard. The old warrior says we should not belittle that animal that is dark as night.

Because whether we believe it or not, the black wolf also has many good qualities: determination, tenacity, courage, strategic thinking. Some of these traits are virtues that the white wolf lacks. Feeding both lets us take advantage of the best of each. It enhances their best version, identifies their needs, and trains us to live in harmony. Let us not starve our fears. It is always better to recognize them, understand them and transform them. Let us not starve our anger, out of our spite or our sadness. Let us not corner them; may we hear what they want to tell us. They can give us valuable lessons on how to be a little better each day.

As we can see, the Cherokee legend of the two wolves teaches a valuable lesson about balance and emotional management. We learn that distributing forces intelligently, feeding both wolves, will give us a better life.

Wolves figure prominently in the mythology of every Native American tribe. In most Native cultures, the wolf is a medicine being associated with courage, strength, loyalty, and success at hunting. Like bears, wolves are closely related to humans by North American tribes, and the origin stories of the Northwest Coast tribes, such as the Quileute and the Kwakiutl, tell of their first ancestors being transformed from wolves into men. In Shoshone mythology, the wolf plays the role of the noble creator god, while in Anishinabe mythology, a wolf character is the brother and true best friend of the culture hero. Among the Pueblo tribes, wolves are one of the six directional guardians, associated with the east and the color white. The Zunis carved stone wolf fetishes are used for protection, ascribing to them both healing and hunting powers. And there you have it, one small look into the very expansive collection of Native American traditions and beliefs.

Chapter IV

The Blue Devil Encounters

The triangle of hills between the towns of Jumbo and Grassy Creek in Webster County, West Virginia is home to the largest cluster of reported sightings of the "Blue Devil." These sightings, which occurred in the winter of 1939-1940, described a bluish, doglike creature, larger than a pony, that prowled the area late at night and emitted a ghostly howl. According to some in Webster County, the animal was responsible for the deaths of a growing number of livestock over the period it stalked the land.

Eventually, the creature began making appearances in neighboring Randolph County. Residents from Randolph joined the Valley Head Rod and Gun Club in offering a $400 reward (over $7,200 today) for the creature's death.

Like other West Virginia counties, Webster County saw a dramatic increase in industrial growth in the early twentieth century. Prior to that time, lack of railroad access kept entrepreneurs from accessing and gathering the vast untapped natural resources of lumber and coal closer to the heart of the state. However, that began to change with the arrival of the Baltimore and Ohio Railroad and West Virginia Midland Railroad in the 1890s and early 1900s.

The forests in the Webster County area were "old growth" forests, meaning they had been undisturbed for well over a century, making them an ideal target for lumber companies. As a result, one of the county's largest and fastest growing industries in the period was the timber industry, and many of the

county's residents made their livelihoods harvesting local lumber. Within a few decades, however, over-harvesting led to the industry's collapse and many area residents were left unemployed. As with many cases of cryptid sightings, economic insecurity fueled individual uncertainties and overactive imaginations, and the "Blue Devil" was born.

One of the first reported sightings of the "Blue Devil" was by Jumbo resident John Clevenger. The former lumber company employee, and then farmer, claimed that his much-valued hunting dog had been attacked and killed by the beast in December 1939. Another farmer, Ernest Cogar, reported that his livestock had been spooked for several nights and some wild animal had attacked and killed one of his cattle and a sheep. Mrs. V.S. Cunlip, meanwhile, reported hearing a "wild, inhuman scream" outside her home in Diana a few miles from Jumbo and H.A. Anderson heard something in Hacker Valley that, "sounded like a panther."

These reports quickly attracted outside attention. Hunters arrived from as close as the county seat of Webster Springs and Buckhannon in neighboring Upshur County, and as far away as the state capital of Charleston and New York City. None of these hunters had any luck finding the beast that allegedly stalked the hills of Webster County. However, the hunters from New York City did have their hunting dogs on the trail of something, but were forced to cut the chase short when their hounds refused to proceed any further.

Newspapers throughout the state, particularly in the state capital of Charleston, reported on the rising panic in the Webster County area with considerable amusement. When the sightings spread to Randolph County in January 1940, the *Charleston Gazette* reprinted a story from the *Elkins Inter-Mountain* calling the beast a "varmint" and wishing it might represent proof positive that panthers still stalked the West Virginia heartlands. Others, particularly locals in Webster and Randolph County, however, were less cynical, and many took part in the growing search for whatever was killing their livestock.

Author Dave Spinks in Webster County overlooking the West Virginia hills where the Blue Devli was said to roam.

WEBSTER SPRINGS
Originally known as Fork Lick for salt springs, known during Revolution, which attracted herds of game. Webster Springs was important health resort for many years. Town retains name of Addison for Addison McLaughlin, owner of its site.

Several claimed to have killed the beast, some seeking to collect the reward offered by the Valley Head Rod and Gun Club. The first, Glen Fisher of Bill Fisher Hollow, reported, before the reward was offered, that he had shot and killed the animal in December 1939, but its body had vanished before he could inspect it in the morning. Another, coal miner Elmer Corley, killed something that Webster County Game Protector C.T. Whittaker character-ized as not a coyote, but resembling one. After collecting the reward, Corley assured area residents that the "Blue Devil" was dead, and no further reports were issued regarding the beast to belie his claim.

The following year, *The Webster Republican* published a story detailing a similar countywide hunt four decades earlier. In 1897, the residents of Web-ster County had participated in the search for, what the paper claimed, was the last known gray wolf in West Virginia. On one night in January 1895, it recounted, the wolf had killed twenty-seven lambs belonging to Jacob Ham-rick in Randolph County. Shortly thereafter, the county courts of Randolph and Webster had offered a $100 reward (a little over $3,000 today). Then, on

New Year's Eve, 1897, the wolf killed five more sheep at John Hamrick's farm near Whitaker's Falls. Banding together, Hamrick and his neighbors set off to hunt for the animal in two feet of snow, stalking it over the course of several days before they finally brought it down. Having published this account shortly after the "Blue Devil" sightings ended in 1940,

The Webster Republican must have hoped its readers would come to the same conclusion it had: that the "Devil" was just one more wild beast like the last gray wolf in West Virginia, nothing supernatural to it. While the *Republican* might have dismissed the "Devil," others haven't. Not surprisingly, many cryptid hunters from around the world are still showing up in Webster County, looking for it. Anyone interested in trying to catch a glimpse of the "Blue Devil" today may try to do so by traveling down scenic Grassy Creek Road in Webster County between Jumbo and Grassy Creek.

The Blue Devil, Other West Virginia Cryptids and the Reporters who covered them

The Following was submitted By
Dr. Raymond Keller

From his book
Cryptids in the West Virginia Paranormal Gallery
© 2022 Dr. Raymond A. Keller of Headline Books, Terra Alta, West Virginia, used by permission of author.

Part I: West Virginia's Dangerous "Blue Devil"

Thanks to the investigations and writings of such famed anomalist investigators as the late John A. Keel of New York (1930-2009) and Gray Barker of West Virginia (1925-1984), West Virginia has become well known as the hotspot for alleged encounters with cryptids of various shapes and sizes. The

From Keller Paranormal Files: In an August 1981 meeting, Harold "Brooksie" Brooks (left) and Webster Republican newspaper (West Virginia) editor and publisher Boyd Dotson (right), reminisce about the infamous "Blue Devil" that appeared in Webster County during the Great Depression.

most famous of these supposed creatures by far is the Mothman, first sighted in the town of Point Pleasant in 1966. And as any Mountaineer can tell you, the Mothman has gone on to become the central figure in numerous books, documentaries, and a 2002 Richard Gere film (*Screen Gems/Sony Pictures*), based on the 1975 book, *Mothman Prophecies* by John A. Keel, *Saturday Review Press*, New York. Among the many other unusual creatures hailing from West Virginia are the Bigfoot, Flatwoods Monster, Grafton Monster, Ogua and Sheepsquatch. All of these have received their fair share of notoriety in the Mountaineer State over the years. However, I now add to these … the Blue Devil and the Rabbit Man. Read on, dear reader….

West Virginia Country Roads Drew Him Home

Back in August 1980, retired Van Nuys, California, mail carrier Harold "Brooksie" Brooks and his wife returned to central West Virginia to visit relatives in his hometown of Webster Springs, the capital of Webster County. Brooks had lived in Van Nuys, California, since 1946, and this was their first trip back to Webster Springs in 34 years. In the late 1930s, Brooks had attained national renown as an early cryptid investigator, writing a series of articles in the Exponent and Telegram newspaper of Clarksburg, West Virginia, about a mysterious, sheep-killing creature roaming about at will in Webster County that was popularly known throughout the West Virginia countryside as the "Blue Devil."

Throughout most of the Great Depression years, Brooks had worked full-time at the A & P grocery store in Webster Springs. Towards the close of the 1930s, he moved on to Cutlips, Inc., a local trucking concern, where he had the opportunity of driving throughout the state. In his spare time, he began his journalistic career by writing about the "Blue Devil" sightings in *The Webster Republican* newspaper, from whence these articles caught the attention of the editor of the larger paper up in Clarksburg. Then, when he would pass through Clarksburg on his trucking delivery route, he would drop off his articles to the editor of the *Exponent and Telegram* newspaper.

When the United States entered World War II in December 1941, patriotic Brooks enlisted in the United States Army Air Corps, where he saw action in the South Pacific theatre of operations. Following the war, he was discharged in California, and liked the climate so much there that he decided to stay. His honorable discharge from military service, helped land him a job with the post office in Van Nuys, in the suburban area of Los Angeles. No sooner than he began working in the post office, he met his future wife; and in the ensuring years in Van Nuys, they raised two daughters, Mary Jo and Paula Sue.

Don't mess with the flocks of a Mountaineer! From Keller Paranormal Files: In the cold winter of 1897, sheep rancher Jacob Hamrick of Whitaker's Falls in Randolph County, West Virginia, rounded up his neighbors and hunted down the "last known gray wolf in the state," believed to be the predator that killed 32 sheep of his flock. Some in central West Virginia in 1939 and 1940 attributed the rampage of the Blue Devil to the appearance of a similar wolf, or maybe a coyote. Others thought the Blue Devil might be some kind of supernatural manifestation.

Upon returning to Webster Springs in 1980, Brooks felt as if he had stepped out of a time machine. There were so many changes. New buildings had popped up everywhere, with many of the old ones having disappeared. Brooks took note that the shrubbery seemed taller, but more trimmed and taken care of, than it was during the Depression years. There were also a lot more businesses and churches. One of the prime characteristics of the city never changed, however, and that was the people. "The people of the city have not changed," remarked Brooks in a local *Webster Republican* newspaper interview, adding that, "Old faces were also missed, especially Mr. J. D.

Cutlip," president of the company he worked for before the war. Both J. D. Cutlip and Boyd Dotson, Sr., had served as a great inspiration for the young Brooks. "They helped me learn the marks of their trades," said Brooks, further declaring that,"They inspired me to be more industrious throughout my life."

Chapter V

The White Thing

White Things, White Devils or Devil Dogs, are among the most historically infamous cryptids in West Virginia. Almost all White Things are described to have dog like features. White creatures are well known to the mountain folk of West Virginia. Like the infamous black mystery dogs, they have roamed these mountains for generations.

While growing up, you hear these stories of these white wolves and dogman like creatures, and you think it's just the old timers trying to scare the beje-sus out of you. But for me, late one night coming home from work, I had a brief but spiritual encounter myself with a giant white wolf.

It was roughly 12:30 a.m. one night in 2009, I was on my way home from working an evening shift from the job I had in law enforcement at that time. I finished my shift at midnight, and I started my hour and fifteen-minute drive home. My drive consisted of heading down Route 5 to Burnsville, W.V. then jumping on Interstate 79 South towards Charleston, W.V. then getting on Route 19 south to Nicholas County, W.V. Once I got on 19, and I reached the base of Pals Mountain, it was extremely foggy. There was so much fog, I had to slow down to about 25 miles an hour with my flashers on so any other drivers could see me and not hit me from behind. It was an eerie dense fog unlike I had ever seen. Visibility was only about ten or fif-teen feet out in front of my truck. As I traversed the long road up the moun-tain, the fog started to dissipate some and my view became much clearer. As I reached the peak of Pals Mountain, out of nowhere, a giant white wolf came out of the fog. It stopped dead in front of my truck, only about 10 feet away. I hit the brakes and came to a complete stop on a four-lane state highway. Thank goodness no one was behind me in either lane. In fact, there were no other vehicles on either side of the highway. This was very odd because this is a heavily traveled state highway. But I was so enamored with this magnificent creature standing in front of me, I didn't realize at the time there were no other people traveling this very busy road.

As I stopped, the wolf turned its head and made eye contact with me. I noticed the wolf's eyes were very yellow and had almost a glowing factor to them. We stared at each other for what seemed like forever, but it was probably only like 20 or 30 seconds. It was a surreal moment, like time stood still. Then just as quickly as the wolf appeared it turned its head, walked across the road, and then disappeared into the darkness. I shook my head, and I think I said out loud, wow, that was crazy. The wolf was enormous. It was twice, maybe even three times the size of any dog I've ever seen. Its upper body was massive and full of muscle. It also had what appeared to be a mane on its back like a lion, and its coat was white as snow with some gray in it. After the encounter, I just continued driving home, thinking to myself how that felt like a supernatural experience in so many ways. For days after, I ran the whole thing over in my head, and all I can take away from it is that it was truly a spiritual moment.

A girl named Dawn Troyer had a terrifying experience one cold night. Dawn was considered pretty, popular, and she was possibly even pregnant. Witnesses placed her in the town pharmacy, purchasing a pregnancy test, soon after the local football team beat their biggest rivals. Danny Chaplin, the high school quarterback, and Dawn were an item. Witnesses saw the two having a heated argument over something unknown, and then the two parted company. It was said that Dawn stormed off tearfully into the darkness, and Danny rejoined his friends for a few beverages.

As morning arrived, Dawn was nowhere to be found, and the town folk began to gather to mount a search for the missing girl. Their attempts at finding the girl turned fruitless, and small rumors began to spread that a strange thing had been going on in this particular neck of the woods. As the towns folk's fears began to reach a fever pitch, they were even more amplified when a man named Delbert Gentry stepped up. He explained how he was out late the previous night for some coon hunting and had spotted the young cheerleader walking along the side of the road. He had offered the girl a ride, but she refused.

 The road through Sandy Huff Hollow was immersed in local lore, a place where it was said the dead were very restless. Only a brave soul would dare traverse the road at night, and Dawn Troyer knew to steer clear of this dreadful place.

Tales of a grim beast, that makes the Hollow its home, were known to everyone from the area. Some say the ghosts that haunt Sandy Huff are the victims of the dreaded beast. They are said to wail in eternal agony over their horrific demise from the claws and fangs of the unspeakable creature. Stories from many hunters say that have spied the beast, often raring up on its hind legs, and tearing through the woods with its dog-like jaws snapping viciously. More than one man has claimed to have been chased from the Hollow by this terrible beast.

On the fourth night of Dawn being missing, Danny decided that he would find her himself. Against the wishes of his friends and family, he trotted off into the woods, with his 12-gauge pump shotgun, in the hopes of finding his girl alive. He did so with the nagging feeling in his gut that something far more sinister had happened to his lost love.

Hours later, the folks of Iaeger, W.V., heard shotgun blasts echoing down from Sandy Huff Hollow. When first light broke, the searchers returned to the woods, but Dawn was still nowhere to be found. Instead, they found the mangled body of Danny Chaplin, his entrails spilled out across the forest floor, his face frozen in abject terror. Clutched in his hand was a ragged and torn remnant from a blue and gold cheerleader uniform, dripping with blood.

In the early days when West Virginia was still known as Western Virginia, the area had more than its share of weird tales of strange and otherworldly creatures seen in the deep dark mountain hollows. One such creature is known as the white werewolf that appears in local folklore.

In the mid-1800s, there was a rash of sightings of a white creature that roamed around the outer woods of French Creek. The townsfolk became frightened as it had been several years since this creature had been sighted in the area. A local farmer claimed that the white monster had killed several of his sheep and escaped after being shot three times. Approximately a month later, the creature was spotted again. This time it was shot at very close range by the farmer's men, only to escape once again. Talk began to spread in the area that the beast was supernatural and could not be killed by any bullet. People feared it was only a matter of time before a person would be killed by its powerful jaws and fangs.

Bill Williams was a well-known wolf hunter. He was known to have killed hundreds of wolves in the area when they were plentiful and caused mayhem on the local livestock. Bill had become a wealthy man by hunting wolves and collecting large bounties on the carcasses of these animals. It was said that Bill had killed so many wolves that he eventually became disgusted by the dirtiness of business and swore that he would never kill another wolf as long as he lived. According to accounts, his view would soon change when the wolf's latest kill was one of Bill's own cows.

As the story goes, Bill set out with his rifle to track the killer wolf and put the town's unrest to bed. Bill brought along a lamb as bait and picked a good spot where he figured the bloodthirsty beast would attack. Waiting in the darkness to lure the wolf in, he figured it would be a quick and easy kill. The townsfolk eagerly awaited the news of Bill's kill, but no word came. It wasn't long before some sought Bill out. To their horror, Bill, the famous wolf hunter, was found dead and the lamb he used for bait was unharmed. It is said that Bill had suffered a gruesome and horrible death as his neck was ripped open, torn away from his body with no trace of blood. No tracks or sign of an attacker of any kind was found anywhere.

To this day, the white wolf is believed to be an avenging entity that killed Bill because he broke his oath to never hunt wolves again. Others feel this was not a wolf and was, in fact, a demonic entity that kills at will whenever it strikes the monster's fancy.

White Wolves continue to be seen all over West Virginia, and stories and accounts tell of how they always escape capture or death by disappearing into the night.

Elkins, West Virginia has been known to have a fair share of white wolf sightings. These sightings seem to always happen during full moons. In these accounts, all attempts to catch or kill one of these wolves has been futile. The beast always seems to return on the full moon, killing and consuming prey at will.

In 2001, a local woman, Vicki Cunningham, said she and her husband had a strange experience. One cold, and snowy night, the couple was driving very late on CR- 151 between Norton and Jim town when to their surprise they spotted a man out walking. As the couple drove past, they turned back to look at the man and were startled to see he had the face of a dog!

West Virginia is a state with dense wilderness areas, farmlands, and is directly in the heart of the Appalachian Mountain chain, which stretches from Georgia to Maine. Tales from over 200 years ago say that a creature of massive size has been roaming the lands searching for blood. The Shawnee Indians claimed it was a shape-shifting werewolf who was out for revenge, but the facts may have been lost to time.

In rural Webster County, West Virginia, a man named Hank and his son, Joe, were riding down one of the many counties back roads, when they caught sight of something utterly amazing. More amazing still is the fact that they not only saw it, but they also actually captured its images on video. They filmed the creature standing near a large dirt mound, and it was taller than the mound itself. The images were a bit fuzzy, as they were taken from the vehicle Hank was driving, while it was in motion. As they rode by, it appeared as if the unknown beast was observing them. Its massive size was evident, as it watched them slowly pass. The video showed the creature squat down and sort of duck behind the large dirt mound for cover. The encounter left both Hank and his son at a loss for words. They had a sense of terror in their hearts that something evil was lurking on their farm, and it was becoming curious.

The legend dates back over 200 years to a time when there was a vast amount of unsettle land in all the states. Much of the area in West Virginia is still as pristine as it was back then, making it an ideal location for a creature such as a werewolf to hide. The Appalachian Mountain Trail (ATC), which starts on Springer Mountain in Georgia and ends on Mt. Katahdin in Maine, runs directly through the area where the video of the Webster County werewolf was filmed. Stories of grass men, sasquatches, and werewolves have been passed down for generations in this area. Until this video, there was no documented proof to the stories, which were usually used as scare tactics to keep unruly children in line.

So, the question remains, what was it that Hank and Joe caught on their digital camera? The images seen are not great, but clearly show a huge creature standing on two legs as they drove by. Some have scoffed at the video, saying it is merely a bear. However, if you look at the image closely, you will notice that while the body could be that of a bear, the head simply doesn't match. The beast is rumored to be seven feet tall and weigh in at well over 400 pounds. These are merely speculations to its size, as no one has ever been lucky enough to capture it, or one of its kindred. As the creature continues to stalk the mountains of West Virginia and the Appalachian Mountains, we can only hope that farmers and hikers alike remain safe.

The names of supernatural beasts and monsters in West Virginia can be confusing. Often, the same or similar names are used to describe different creatures, and in most cases, it seems to vary from county to county. As is the case of the White Thing of West Virginia, it is often described by eyewitnesses as basically a giant white wolf, but it is also said to be a hellhound. In most historical accounts hellhounds are described to be as black as coal, however in West Virginia The White Thing is also described as being a hellhound by some accounts.

They are said to resemble wolves, bears, cows, and even huge badgers of various colors and are as large as a lion in some reports. The hair is long and shaggy, snow-white and somewhat dirty at times. Their jaws are immense, with very large fangs to boot. They are swift and move at lighting speed, sometimes on two legs rather than four like most known wolves. In other reports, they have more than four legs. They have been known to emit a chilling scream that sounds, to some, what they think a woman being murdered would sound like. The monster attacks without provocation. Many victims of these attacks describe the feeling of their fangs ripping through their flesh only, to discover that once the attack is over there is not a mark on their bodies. They then realize the attack must have been supernatural in nature. The white thing is known to rip animals apart in similar fashion to reports of werewolf attacks, in that their throats are torn out, and the corpses are left bloodless, with no blood found near the bodies. In some reports, there are variations in the descriptions of the monster. Some folks call them "White Devils" because they have glowing red eyes, walk on two legs, with long sharp claws. Some are known to have ties to cemeteries and are also considered to be omens of death.

In 1973, a strange white creature was seen in the TNT area of Point Pleasant by a seven-year-old boy. While riding in the car with his family, he saw something white with shaggy hair, and it had a head that was some 3 feet wide, according to his description. It floated alongside the car in the air, following the family for just a few moments at speeds of up to 65 miles an hour.

Another interesting encounter at the farm, happened over 20 years ago. A couple, who were driving home from a party, saw the White Wolf themselves. As they were passing the front of the farm, they decided to stop near the property to fool around a bit. As the two were sitting there with the car lights off, in pitch darkness, the woman saw a white form moving around the outside of their car. She thought it was just her eyes playing tricks on her in the darkness, until she noticed the thing standing right outside of their car. The creature then let out a blood-curdling howl that was so loud it sent shivers down their spines. She noticed that the thing was staring right at them. Paralyzed by fear, the woman couldn't move. Her boyfriend fumbled with the keys in fright, trying to flee. Finally, he got the car started and tore out of there, never slowing down until they were well clear of the farm.

For many years, the locals in Ragland, W.V. have talked about the "White Thing". This small community outside of Delbarton, in Mingo County, knows this creature very well. A group of longtime friends have talked about their encounters with this creature on many occasions. One of them said it could stand up on two legs like a man and was exceptionally tall, over 7 feet, and it could run faster than anything he had ever seen, including deer. Two of the others were riding an ATV near the railroad tracks just before dark and saw it run right across in front of them on four legs. The creature, on two legs, then jumped up on a stack of railroad ties that are at least 4 and a half feet tall. It then leaped another 10 feet up onto the hillside. When the two of them returned home, they were extremely shaken and could barely get the story out of what they had experienced. Some of the town folk there believe this beast is related to some sort of satanic worship that was said to have taken place near 24 Hollow, close to a battery shop in Ragland, but no one knows for sure.

These White Things have been reported all over the state. One significant account happened when an unidentified hunter was out in the West Virginia wilderness with some friends. They were making their way along a remote trail, when they say a hairy white animal like a large, white dog, with a bushy tail, pounced upon them out of nowhere. They reported that the creature issued a bloodcurdling scream that echoed all over the area. Whatever this thing was, it knocked the hunter down, over the hill that the group was on. Bewildered at what had just happened to him, the man began screaming in pain and fear. When the rest of the group reached their friend, he was out of his mind, screaming that the monster had ripped him apart and his guts were out of his body. Doing a quick inspection of their friend, assessing his injuries, the group noticed there wasn't a mark on his body. The others saw the creature attack their friend, and for the life of them, they could not figure out why there wasn't even a scratch on the man. So, what exactly is going on with this White Thing, is it a real flesh and blood creature? Or is it something even more terrifying, a supernatural being that can interact with the living?

A similar account was reported in 1929 by a man named Frank Kozul, who was headed home through a wooded area known as Morgan's Ridge, in Fairmount, West Virginia. While traversing the thick woods, his trip was interrupted by the sight of a strange creature standing not far ahead in his path. He described the creature as being an extremely large dog, with a huge head, powerful jaws, a bushy tail, and covered in snow-white fur. As soon as the thing spotted Frank, it pounced on him, biting, and clawing him relentlessly, but surprisingly causing no physical damage to him. Frank punched and kicked the creature tirelessly, but his efforts were in vain as his attempts seemed to hit nothing, as if he was punching and kicking at air. He knew the creature had a mass of some sort because its weight was able to knock him to the ground when it pounced upon him. The beast made no sound whatsoever as it attacked him, as Frank recalled hearing bird sounds and other forest sounds while he was being attacked.

Here we have two reports of a similarly described creature that caused no physical marks upon its victims, even though it was able to knock them both to the ground.

Another person who had an experience while hiking a remote trail in West Virginia reported seeing a large horned creature crawl out of some underbrush. The hiker said the creature had a brownish white coat and smelled of sulfur so putrid that he gagged from it. It moved on all fours as he watched it kneel to drink water from the creek. The front limbs were paw-like hands. Its head was long and shaped like that of a canine, and it had large horns, not antlers. He watched it drink for a few minutes, and then it crossed through the creek, continuing towards Sand Hill Road. The witness, terrified at what he saw, ran away as fast as he could muster to his car.

One more account comes from a woman we will call "Melanie," for privacy purposes. Melanie was driving down a very isolated country road with her husband one night, when they saw a creature crouching on the road, approximately 50 yards ahead of the couple. It was on all fours and was pure white in color. It was much bigger than any dog they had ever seen. As the two got closer, it turned and looked directly at them and suddenly, its mouth went open. It stood up on two legs, began running across the road, up into the woods and out of sight. Neither one of the couple said a word at first until the husband asked the wife if she had seen what he saw, and that's when the woman began to cry.

When it comes to sightings and encounters with the infamous White Thing of West Virginia, descriptions vary greatly in size, appendages, and features but at least one thing remains constant, the white colored fur on these spectral creatures.

In some reports, it seems to be described as more like something that could be like a Bigfoot, but it differs greatly in most aspects than your standard Bigfoot description.

One report that came in from Bakers Ridge, involved a college student who was house sitting for some friends. Late one night, he began hearing some loud banging sounds coming from the back porch. Thinking it was just a raccoon rummaging around on the porch, she paid no attention to it for a little while. As she went to check it out, she noticed red glowing eyes peering back at her. The creature stood around five feet in height and began rushing at the house, throwing its body against it, while letting out ferocious howling noises. Still watching the creature and afraid to move out of sheer fright, she noticed the creature was covered in long matted white hair and had human like hands. After quite sometime, the creature seemed to give up and slunk out of sight into the woods.

When it comes to the White Thing of West Virginia, this creature is very malevolent in nature, often lashing out and attacking unsuspecting people. However, it is extremely strange at how it often leaves no physical damage upon its victims. Although, when one experiences the wrath of this creature, it is certain to leave a long-lasting, life-changing impression upon the folks that have an encounter with it.

Chapter VI

The Snarly Yow, Devil Dogs, Hell Hounds and Black Dog Legends and Encounters of West Virginia

To better understand some of these monsters that are said to lurk within the borders of the Mountain State, we must first learn a little about the habitat that these creatures are thought to reside in. Take the Monongahela National Forest, for example, it was established in 1911 following the Weeks Act. The main purpose of the Weeks Act was to establish long-term protection of watersheds, and natural resources following the mass cutting of eastern forests in the late 19th and 20th centuries. Early on, in 1915, the Monongahela Purchase encompassed 7200 acres and by the end of 1924, it became known as the Monongahela National Forest and grew to 150,367 acres. Today it covers an astounding 921,000 acres or 1,439 sq miles. As one can see, this is a vast, rugged area of high mountains and deep valleys. In fact, there are some places in the forest so remote and rugged that people rarely attempt to traverse it. This is due to the inherent dangers as well as lack of any immediate help that may be required in case of an emergency.

The geography of the area consists of parts of the Allegheny Mountain Range, which is but a small section of the vast Appalachian Mountain range, and lies entirely in the state of West Virginia. The Forest has varying elevations from 900 feet to 4,863 feet at Spruce Knob. It boasts a wide array of weather conditions due to the way the mountains are situated. On the west side of the mountains, the forest boasts an annual rainfall amount of 60 inches, compared to 30 inches on the East side. The forest is the home of the headwater of six major river systems: the Monongahela River, Greenbrier River, Potomac River, Elk River, Gauley River, and Tygart River. There are 12 more rivers that have been included in a study to see if they too are part of this vast water shed.

Not only is the geology of the area important, when it comes to researching this monster phenomena, in this forest, but even more important is the ecology. It is noted for its ruggedness, breathtaking views, blueberry and blackberry thickets, highland bogs, sods and massive open areas with exposed rock cliffs. A whole host of botanicals can be found in the forest including second growth trees throughout, along with cactus on the east side, as well as laurel, and rhododendron on the west side of the mountains.

There are over 230 known species of birds that live in the Monongahela Forest. Among others, there are nine endangered species that inhabit the area including one species of flying squirrel, two bat species, one salamander species and two bird species. There are 50 other species of rare plants and animals also found within its borders.

Big game species are also abundant throughout the forest including black bear, white-tailed deer, wild turkey, gray and fox squirrels, rabbits, snowshoe hare, woodcock, and grouse. A wide array of fur-bearing animals also call the area home, such as the bobcat, fisher, raccoon, river otter, and mink. Also skunks, opossums, woodchucks, coyote, crows, and weasels live in these woods. Plenty of fish also inhabit the vast water systems that flow within the forest, 12 species of panfish and over 60 species of forage fish. Over 90% of West Virginia's trout waters lie within the forest borders. Another interesting fact is that there is a small area of 318 acres that still holds old-growth forest. There is also a vast cave system in and around the forest that provides shelter to many different animal species that live there. All these factors are significant in our search for these monsters. Let's not forget that it is very rural and the number of people that live and work in the forest is significantly low.

For a creature such as this to survive it must have three things and those are water, food and some sort of shelter. Of course, that is barring that it is not some sort of extraterrestrial or supernatural being and doesn't require the same things that most mammals need to survive. Any 5th grader can see that this forest could support such an animal for a significant period. Not only in small numbers, but a large number could indeed survive in the forest for some time.

We also know that any species needs a breeding population to survive, and that is one of the major questions researchers are looking into. Again, that's assuming it's like other animals and must procreate to carry on the species.

Snarly Yow

The Legend of the Snarly Yow is about a black dog known to haunt the Eastern Panhandle of West Virginia. It is said to be jet black in color, with a fierce mouth, glowing eyes, and large paws. This canine like animal is named after a legend, that originated in Wales hundreds of years ago. It makes sense that, since many European settlers who came to the area brought their folklore and tales of devilish creatures lurking among us with them to West Virginia. Sightings are still being reported here to this day.

Although many of the reports stem from the South Mountain area in Maryland, the creature's range extends as far south as Hillsboro, Virginia, and parts of West Virginia, especially in and around Harpers Ferry. It makes perfect sense that it is the same creature that's been seen all over West Virginia,

Historical marker in Boonsboro, Md. that has a recounting of an encounter with a Snarly Yow.

as there are no border fences that would keep this creature from crossing back and forth into one state or another.

In the early 1900s, many travelers reported seeing a massive black dog that confronted them, scarring them nearly to death. Interestingly enough, the creature never attacked or hurt anyone. Many people who encountered the creature attempted to kill it. All efforts failed. Many bullets were said to simply pass right through the beast without causing any harm or leaving a blood trail.

There is a Civil War historical marker in Boonsboro, Maryland, with a sidebar briefly recounting an encounter with the Snarly Yow:

Legend has it that the shadow of a black dog used to prowl the heights of South Mountain. One night, a huntsman, famous as a sure shot, encountered the beast. He aimed and fired his rifle. The shot went right through the animal with no effect. He fired again, and again, each shot passing through the shadowy beast. Finally overcome with dread, the huntsman fled.

The Snarly Yow has been spotted in the mountains and hills near Harpers Ferry, part of West Virginia's Eastern Panhandle. The stories of the Snarly Yow here begin in the 1700s, when the first Germans settled in the Potomac Valley. The name comes from the Germanic words to describe this creature's howls and wails. Innumerable accounts have been told by West Virginians of the Snarly Yow being hit by cars and getting back up with no injuries, and simply disappearing in front of people.

The town of Harpers Ferry was hotly contested and changed hands many times during the Civil War. The bloodiest battle of the War Between the States took place in nearby Sharpsburg, Maryland. The Battle of Antietam claimed over 22,000 casualties in a single day of combat. Many ghost stories are set in the area near the Antietam Battlefield. Many stories of the appearance of the Snarly Yow also have plagued the area.

 South Mountain, on the border of West Virginia, in Maryland, is said to be the home of the Snarly Yow. It is believed that the bloodshed from the war is the reason the creature lurks in the area. The area sits on a ley line and many mysterious things have been reported in and around the region, even predating the war.

In the early 1900s, hundreds of people reported seeing a gigantic beast that resembled a dog except for the size of the creature, its massive paws and an ugly red mouth. Horses, like the people, were afraid of the creature. It would suddenly appear on the road, confront travelers, then vanish before the astonished onlookers. After an untold number of reports around the turn of the century, sightings dwindled to nothing for many years, until the summer of 1975 when it was seen again by credible witnesses.

A man named William was returning home to his family one night when he encountered the black beast known as the Snarly Yow. He was known as a sober and strong man by his friends and family. After finishing his work for the day, he approached the area called Glendale. He saw the creature come into view and stand in the center of the road, blocking his path. He described the thing as bigger than any dog he had ever seen. Bewildered at the sight of the creature, he decided to try to scare it away by throwing rocks and sticks at it. But instead of the thrown objects hitting the dog like creature, they passed right through it, having no effect. The Snarly Yow soon snarled and barred its teeth at William. Then, with no rhyme or reason, it turned and continued off the road into the brush.

A man, known to area residents as one of the best sharpshooters in the area, also came upon the Snarly Yow. He took aim with his rifle and fired several well-directed shots at the animal, but each bullet passed through the beast, leaving no mark. He soon fled, shaken and terrified at the ordeal.

While on horseback, a character who went by the name of "Big Joe," due to his gigantic stature, came across the Black Dog on horseback while riding on a trail. The dog started running, and Big Joe gave chase. During the heat of the chase, it just suddenly vanished.

A man who was causing a ruckus at an entertainment event was about to be arrested, when he evaded the authorities, mounted his steed and headed home. Seeing the Black Dog, he spurred his horse, but the horse became spooked at the sight of the creature and bucked the man off, breaking his collarbone.

After the historical rash of sightings in the early 20th century, the sightings dwindled to almost nothing. Then in the 1970s it started all over again when a new wave of sightings began to pour in.

During the new round of Snarly Yow encounters, motorists began reporting a dog that would suddenly appear in front of their cars. In 1976, a couple reported hitting a large, bluish-black dog with glowing eyes. When they stopped to investigate, it had vanished without a trace. Other motorists have

Many stories of the appearance of the Snarly Yow have plagued the area of Antietam Battlefield, located in Sharpsburg, Md., the scene of the bloodiest battle of the Civil War. .

hit the creature after it materialized in front of their car, only to have their vehicle pass through it and see the creature standing in the road behind them.

In the 1970s, a man, who became startled by the appearance of the creature, began throwing rocks and sticks at it. Each rock he threw passed right

Author Dave Spinks at Harpers Ferry, the scene of many Snarly Yow sightings for hundreds of years.

through its body. The creature glared at its attacker and snarled before disappearing into the brush.

A visiting minister, returning along a local road, after holding evening prayer near Glendale, claimed to have seen the dog on several occasions.

Still yet another account talks about a carload of people who saw a black dog appear in front of them. Unable to stop in time, they all felt the thud of the car hitting the animal, heard it being jolted, rattled, and crushed underneath the car. They stopped and started to get out of the car, when one of them spotted the huge black dog standing in the road showing its teeth to them. The creature then disappeared right in front of their eyes.

Just a few years ago, while walking alone, a man heard what he thought was a dog run up next to him. He went to pet the dog, yet nothing was there. He said that he remembers for certain that he could hear the dog panting. Not only that, but he sped up his pace, and the dog that wasn't there kept pace with him, and as he rounded a curve the activity simply stopped.

In the case of the Snarly Yow, there seems to be enough evidence, through historical data, that there is something going on. This beast is more of an apparition rather than a living, breathing creature. Eyewitnesses have seen them vanish into thin air before their very eyes, glide right through fences without being affected. Some have seen bullets pass through them without effect, and more.

The phantom Black Dog is found in West Virginia folklore. Unlike the Black Dog of British folklore, the Snarly Yow is sometimes described not as black, but as a white headed dog dragging a chain from its neck. It has a red mouth, glowing eyes and over-sized paws and known to be very intimidating in appearance. A few sightings will claim the beast stands on its hind legs or that it can change its size to that of a small pony.

British Black Dog

In England and Scotland, there is a ton of folklore regarding Black Dogs. Sightings of these dogs have been going on for over 400 years. In British folklore, seeing a Black Dog is often an omen of death. These Black Dogs are typically found out in the wilderness along old roads, bridges, and pathways. Like the Snarly Yow, the British Black Dogs have glowing red eyes, are large and able to change their size; suddenly appearing and vanishing. While some Black Dogs are more vicious than others, it is only if they come into physical contact with someone that they attack. Could it be that these creatures followed early settlers here? It stands to reason that the early settlers most definitely brought their folklore here from Europe.

The animal that is reported in the states, specifically in West Virginia, Maryland, and Virginia, is different from that of the English variety. It is not an omen of death, but instead it just appears, blocks the road and disappears just as quickly.

Hellhounds

Robert Johnson's song, "Hellhound on My Trail," is considered one of the most haunting songs of all time. It is widely thought that he made a deal with the devil at the crossroads because he disappeared for quite some time, and then reappeared a much more accomplished musician than previously known. It is believed that he wrote that song because he knew his days were numbered, and the devil would soon be sending his hellhounds to collect the debt of Robert's soul. The association between black dogs and the nether world is vastly known by many different peoples and cultures around the world. These hellish hounds are associated with bad omens, the Devil, death, and the crossroads demon.

It's of no surprise that when early settlers came to Appalachia, they brought that folklore with them. Many writers have told narratives of supernatural or devil dogs in the tales from the Appalachia region because of the simple fact early settlers of the region stem from areas in Europe that these tales came from.

In the early days, whenever one of these creatures was spotted, groups of young and experienced hunters were put together to keep a lookout for the black dogs. Some who saw it, as well as others, believed it to some kind of witch.

Seeing a hellhound or hearing one howl may be an omen or even a cause of death. Hellhounds are called The Bearers of Death because ancient demons supposedly created them to serve as heralds of death. According to legend, seeing one leads to a person's death. Some legends say you only need to see it once. Others say it requires three sightings for the curse to take effect and kill the victim. These factors make the Hellhound a feared symbol of bad things that are about to happen.

Guardians and Gatekeepers

They often get assigned to guard the entrances to the world of the dead, such as graveyards and burial grounds, or undertake other duties related to the afterlife or the supernatural. Hellhounds not only are guards for cemeteries, but they are frequently seen as helper dogs for those who are about to pass. But they also can show up to said loved ones to inform them of a loved one's passing.

Appearance & Abilities

Hellhounds have been said to be as black as coal and smell of burning brimstone. They tend to leave behind a burned area wherever they go. Their eyes are a deep, bright, and almost glowing red.

Other features that have been attributed to hellhounds include glowing red – or sometimes yellow – eyes, razor sharp teeth, super strength, or speed, ghostly or phantom characteristics, foul odor, and sometimes even the ability to talk. In cultures that associate the afterlife with fire, hellhounds may have fire-based abilities and appearance.

Chapter VII

Recent

W.V. Sightings and Encounters

One account, I recall well, comes out of an area near my home and just a few miles from the Dave Spinks World of Weird store in Richwood, West Virginia. It comes from an area known as Cranberry Ridge that lies within Monongahela National Forest. I know this area very well, as I have hunted the area off and on during my life. I have also conducted investigations in and around the area over my thirty plus years of investigating the strange and unexplained.

Many years after the Blue Devil Encounters, two cousins and their fathers, joined a group of hunters at a deer camp on Cranberry Ridge near the Webster County and Nicholas County Line. The camp lies deep in the woods, well off the beaten path. The day was warm, and a heavy rain had set in. The cousins, their father and uncle soon realized they had forgotten some supplies that they needed to cook with. So, the two young cousins volunteered to head over to the Nicholas County side and pick up the supplies the group needed to prepare their meals. The boys dawned their rain gear and headed over the ridge. As they neared the Gauley River, the rain began to let up. The cloud cover opened overhead and soon moonlight became visible. There were big mudholes and the boys soon found themselves stuck in one. They jumped off their all-terrain vehicle and pushed it loose from the deep mud. As they took a break, they began to remove their rain gear and check the gas level in the ATV. One of the boys noticed an enormous wolf standing there on its hind legs behind them on the trail. Being that it was dark, the beast was only visible by its silhouette. The boy went on to describe the creature as having long pointed ears, a long dog like snout, it was covered in hair and stood around 7 feet tall. He finally got up enough muster to tell his cousin to look. His cousin turned and saw the creature standing there eyeballing them. The two quickly jumped on the ATV and took off as fast as they could go, never looking back out of sheer fright. Finally, making back to the uncle's house, they shared their terrifying encounter with their aunt and refused to go back to the camp alone. After some time, the aunt had them load the ATV up in the back of a pickup truck, and she drove them back to the camp.

Going back to the Blue Devil Encounters of the 1930s in Webster County, it was reported that the beast was killed. If so, why are there still accounts being reported in and around the same area, some fifty or more years later? One can only guess, but you can bet there will be more sightings and encounters to come.

Werewolf of Lincoln County

During the Spring of 1980, around 4 p.m., while hiking in Lincoln County, West Virginia, a young couple came across a creature that terrified them and defied everything they thought they knew about animals in the woods. As they traversed a steep and narrow trail, they heard what they thought was a bear approaching them in a nearby thicket of brush. They could not see what was causing the racket due to the thickness of the brush, and simply assumed it was a bear. It was common for folks to see bears in this area, so they thought nothing of and just remained motionless in the hopes of avoiding contact with the bear.

To their surprise and dismay, the creature suddenly stepped out of the brush and onto the trail a mere thirty yards in front of them. This thing was no bear, it was black in color and larger than any bear they had ever seen or heard of. It sported a long snout like a wolf, a long bushy tail and pointed long ears. The witnesses claimed it stunk with a horrible odor. As the creature lumbered along on all fours, the man quietly but quickly positioned himself in front of his girlfriend. That's when it stopped and stood up on its hind legs, towering over the couple at 7 feet or more in height, as it stared at them with glowing red eyes. At that moment, the couple feared they were going to be attacked. But just as quickly as it happened, the monster walked off into the woods and was gone. The two did notice that the front legs appeared to be noticeably shorter than the hind legs and looked more like arms than legs.

Upon returning home, the young man reported the encounter to his father, who grew up in the woods of West Virginia himself. The father told his son that he had heard about this thing when he was a young boy back in the 1930s and 40s. He told of how the monster would prowl around surrounding homesteads and farms, killing and eating the livestock. He told his son that family dogs were petrified of it and would often crawl deep under the house when the creature was wandering around the farms looking for its next meal. People would talk of how the very ground would shake as it walked around peering in windows, and no one would dare venture out of the house when it was spotted nearby. Usually in the morning after it was seen, they would find a dead cow or horse partially consumed with deep lacerations across their bodies and their throats would be ripped out. No one ever knew what this creature was or where it came from, but for generations this creature or others like it have been reported in the Lincoln County wood.

In 1995, at approximately 7:30 p.m., a man was returning home from a martial arts class near Morgantown, W.V. Just short of Masontown, an enormous dog like creature leapt from the cliff, alongside the roadway, on the driver's side of the car. He hit the brakes and stopped. The creature stood in the center of the road, barring its teeth as it snarled. Feeling as if it were about to lunge and attack, the man was frozen, awed by the creature. Suddenly, a car appeared from the opposite direction. The driver must have seen the thing as well, because the car also came to a screeching halt. That's when the beast jumped from the middle of the road, clearing the lane, and went over the embankment in a single leap.

Another encounter that I have investigated was that of a well-known prose-cuting attorney's son here in West Virginia. I cannot say what county this occurred in due to privacy concerns. The encounter occurred in 2020 on a fall night .It happened one night while the son and his friend were riding four wheelers at night. While riding some of the normal trails the boys often utilized, they came upon a spot where there was a tight turn on the trail where an old, decrepit boat was abandoned deep in the woods many years ago. As the boys slowed to make the turn the prosecutors' sons' headlights on his four-wheeler shone on the old boat. There, standing behind the boat was what he described as an enormous werewolf standing on two legs. The creature was grey and black in color with a dog like snout and glowing red eyes. The boy said that almost as soon as the lights from the ATV illuminat-ed the thing, that the dogman quickly squatted down behind the boat as if it was trying hide from the lights. Not wasting anytime due to fearing for his life, he mashed the throttle on his machine and raced out of the area travel-ing nearly two miles before stopping. Once he felt he was safe, he stopped with his friend in tow. The two discussed with one another what they had seen. Upon realizing they both described seeing a 7-foot-tall werewolf like creature they became even more frightened and returned home immediately telling the boy's father about what they had just encountered.

They next day the boy's father contacted me via email, and it was a short time later that I was on the phone with the pair. After interviewing the boy for over an hour, I instructed them to return to the site to try and see if there was any sign of the creature in or around the general area where the boys saw the thing standing. I asked them to take pictures of the area and look for any track signs or hair of any sort of thing that may have been lost or shed by the creature. I instructed them to bag anything they found and get back to me right away if anything whatsoever was discovered.

As fate would have it, a heavy rain set in that day and the pair were not able to return to the site until the rain had subsided. Once the rain left the area, the father and son returned and surveyed the site for a significant amount of time. They found no sign, except one suspect indention in the soft mud that could have been a track, but the rain had essentially made it unreadable.

As with any investigation, with no hard evidence reported, encounters are simply just a story. As with many stories of this nature we must take them with a grain of salt. As investigators, we cannot simply discount the stories because we weren't there. We must consider the nature and the character of the of the individuals sharing the accounts before discounting them. We also must take a close, hard look at the sheer number of these accounts in a particular area or state, and use that information to warrant further investigations into the phenomenon. After all supernatural events don't exactly follow the scientific model.

The Following accounts were submitted
By Joedy Cook
Founder of the North American Dogman Project

In 2002, a 32-year-old woman from Hancock County had a compelling encounter. She was residing on the farm where she had lived since she was ten years old. Her mom was very fond of horses, and she was finally able to live out her dream by raising horses on their farm. One night, around 2 a.m., she heard a knock on the door. Having lived on a farm most of her life, she knew that someone knocking on the door, that late at night, usually meant something bad had happened. It was her neighbor letting her know that some of the horses had gotten out and were in his yard. Her stepfather got up and asked her what was going on. When she told him about the horses getting out, he said they were her horses, so she could deal with it. Being that she was still half asleep, she had forgotten to ask the neighbor what yard the horses were in. Being that this group of horses had a few escape artists in it, she had the routine down pat.

It was a dark night, with the only light coming from a little amount of moonlight and small motion light that had a limited distance. The woman was very upset as she walked outside, cursing at the horses for escaping and her having to go out and fetch them. The following is her account of what happened next.

I was naturally in a foul mood, cursing my horses, and wondering if some drunk had gone through the fence, AGAIN. It happened a lot. As I got closer to the brown barn, I realized a horse was flipping out. It was running back and forth, squealing, and carrying on. I went in and grabbed the halters and leads. I paused for a moment, to see if any other horse or horses had replied to the horse. If I heard a squeal, that would give me an idea where the other horse or horses might be. There was no reply. That was odd. I was thinking, "Crap! They're on the other side of the hill!" It was the only reason in my mind they wouldn't be replying. Let's just say, when they followed our cut trails, to the other side, it took us an hour to traverse through the woods and lead them back. And even with two guys, on a four-wheeler, and my mom, that was a freaky trek.

I felt like I was being watched and followed. Maybe, it wasn't paranoia.

So the land is set up like this, the brown barn was connected to a small pasture, about half an acre long, which then connects to a seven-acre pasture. Pretty much in the center, on the outside edge of the large pasture, was an old, white barn, that we turned into a run-in.

I decided to tackle the horse still in the fence, so I could bring her down to the small pasture, to keep her from escaping too. Maybe, the others would follow. I had to walk clear to the other side of the pasture, to get to the panicking horse. It was my mother's psycho appaloosa mare. I tried to catch her and nearly got trampled, a few times trying. She was frothing at the mouth and her eye whites were REALLY showing! Was I alarmed? No. As I said, psycho!

I noticed my other six were across the road. They were standing in a tiny, little fenced-in area, under a spotlight. They were standing motionless and not touching a blade of grass. I wondered how the neighbor managed to herd them into that tiny fenced in area, with that tiny door. Three of those horses were over sixteen hands tall. One was a draft horse cross. The doorway was small enough; he touched both sides, going through. My thoroughbred mare took me two hours to corral, the last time she got out (much to my frustration, she was an awesome jumper). So, a stranger rounding them up and putting them into a tiny yard was mind-blowing.

I've had horses since I was nine. I'm thirty-two now. I've had ponies and horses. I've had appaloosas, Arabians, draft horses, quarter horses, walking horses, saddle reds, thoroughbreds, mustangs, foals, geldings, mares, and geldings that still thought they were stallions. I've had a lot of horses, from all walks of life. I will tell you; they consistently do not like to be crammed into tight spaces, especially, not in a group.

I had two severely abused horses. I was rehabbing, a thoroughbred that had PTSD, and a racking horse, that actually took me three years to touch, without some sort of a bad reaction. They did not like being in stalls, and all but one were female. Mares are extremely moody, and two of mine were particularly vicious to those they didn't like. My walker mare only liked three other horses. She should have been kicking the crap out of the others there. Mine also didn't like to be under lights when they escaped. They avoided them like the plague. And not eating grass, that was over ankle deep? That was unheard of. They were silent and dead still.

My neighbor came out and told me that they were like that when he found them. He asked me if I needed help, but I said, "No." My thoroughbred and racking horse mares did not like men. I told him I'd take them out, one at a time. I took one halter and lead and threw the rest outside the gate. I put the halter on my gelding and opened the gate to lead him out. They had other plans, though. All six came out, as a freaking unit. They were literally chest to butt, crammed together. My gelding and my Welsh mare had their chest pushing against me as we walked back to the brown barn. Normally, they did not do this. I wouldn't usually allow such bad behavior.

We were on the main road, which I did not like. The speed limit is only 35, but people go 60. So, I tried to lead them through the large pasture gate. They wouldn't even go on that side of the road. I was a little unnerved, by their behavior. So, I lead them down to the brown barn, and they went in. They were skittish, though, picking at the hay I threw out, walking around restlessly, sticking to the barn like glue, and eyeing the upper pasture. I rationalize it by thinking, it's the appy flipping out, that's unnerving them. And why hadn't she come down yet? She had to have seen us all walk down. I rushed to the gate, between the little and big pastures, out of habit. I didn't want the herd to go back out, into the big pasture. I didn't have to worry. They didn't follow me (like they usually did). The gate was wide open, but the appy was still running and squealing, back and forth, in the same area. I started to go get her.

Now, the neighbors' security lights didn't really light up my pasture. The road was higher than my pasture, so it was cast in a shadow. I could make out her shape and some detail, though. She took off, at a panicked gallop, swerved sideways, and jumped the stream. When she landed, she nearly landed on her face. She caught herself though and took off at a dead gallop again. I ducked behind a stump. If she would have hit me, I would have been dead.

I went back and chained the gate. I decided to forego looking her over until I got the halters and leads. She was too hot now. I decided to walk on the road, instead of through the pasture, again. The pasture was uneven, unlit, and full of springs. Sometime during this, clouds had taken over the sky, so, there was no moonlight, to see by. The spot, on the road, where I was at, was paved and well lit, since my neighbor was paranoid as already mentioned.

I had almost gotten to the white barn, when I got this sudden urge to stop and look at a very specific spot in the pasture. I would like to say, it was instinct that told me to look, but usually, I'd scan the woods first, to see what was watching me. That's usually where the watchers are. Instead, I just flicked on my flashlight, right on a certain spot. It was extremely close to where the mare was flipping out. I saw red eye shine. My first thought was, "Why in the world would a deer be there, with all that chaos?" I was feeling a sense of extreme dread and didn't know why. Besides, it being where my horse was going nuts, told me, something else just wasn't right. I then realized, where the eyes were, relative to the walnut trees and my racing barrels. See, the road is above the pasture and the walnut trees were right at the same elevation as the road. The pasture itself is sloped, to deal with the runoff from the road. The barrel, it was next to, was on the low end of the incline. The barrels were white, so I could see a dim lighting (from my flashlight) on the one it was next to. This thing was too freaking big to be a deer.

I was frozen, standing there, watching it. I just had this feeling, it was evil and that I had to keep track of those eyes. It was watching me. It slowly blinked a few times. It also looked over, into the woods, above the pasture. I know you ask your guests if they ever feel there are other ones out there, well, let me tell you, it crossed my mind. With a sinking stomach, I flashed my flashlight over the woods, to see if I would catch eyeshine. I didn't see any, so I went right back to the eyes. They were still there. I flicked back and forth, making sure nothing was sneaking up on me.

I don't know how long I stood there, watching, frozen. Someone could have come around the bend and hit me with their car, I was so focused. Finally, it started to move off. It glanced at me, sideways, a few times, with only one eye. I think it went into the copse of trees, around the creek. I heard nothing. That wasn't surprising, though. The horses were still restless and making noises. I stood there, a long time after, looking for eye shine. I was wondering if it could have been a bear. I didn't think so, though. The eyes were consistent, in height, until it disappeared. Bears are clumsy, on their back legs. On this uneven, inclined ground, I have no doubt a bear would have dropped to the ground, to go on all fours. Even the rear up and drop-down behavior bears do, when they're trying to see something, wouldn't work. We had one cross our pasture before. He made a lot of noise going through the woods. The horses settled down quicker with the bear.

I was almost to my neighbor's at this point. I considered leaving the couple of hundred dollars of tack at his house (halters and leads aren't cheap). I had no doubt, if I left them there, they'd be gone in the morning. My mother would be pissed. So, I darted over, grabbed them, and ran like a bat out of hell! I know. I know. I should have left the tack. I also know, you're not supposed to run, but I couldn't even conceive what I had just seen. I got into the barn, threw the tack down, and hung with the horses. I wasn't going to go back up that pitch-black driveway on foot. I figured, with the horses, I'd have a warning, and the barn had plenty of sharp things. I didn't go back up, until dawn. I was frozen stiff by that time.

I've had years to think this over. It unnerves me to no end. How long was that thing there? Was that what was keeping the appy mare from coming down? Was it RIGHT there, in the shadows, while I was trying to catch her or was it in the unlit barn I walked through, to get to the road? Was it the reason the appy swerved and nearly fell? How did my horses get out? I never did find how they got out. Did they panic and jump the fence? I did check the fence line, away from the woods. I did look for tracks, around the barrel. Sadly, the ground was hard, from frost that morning. But I will say, the appy mare was running for a good while. The ground was severely torn up and turned into a muddy mess (it was high noon when I went down there, to check, and the ground had melted). I'll bet it was her, that woke the neighbor up. It took them about a week, to fully settle. I don't know if, whatever it was, was still in the area or if they were that traumatized.

It wasn't long after that, my mother filed for divorce. My ex-stepfather got the farm and I moved in with her, in the city. Even with all the weird crap going on there (there were non-bipedal things going on too), I miss it terribly. Maybe it's more accurate to say, I miss the farm life rather than the actual place. I'd love to get back onto a farm again, but I'd probably hesitate to move back there.

I never told anyone about the eye shine event. I didn't see the actual creature and really, how do you convey that unnatural/horror inducing feeling? You saw eye shine, whoop-dee-doo. My mother would have given me the benefit of the doubt, but my mother often told family members things. They made my life enough of a living hell. I didn't want to give them more ammo.

"My name is Ronald. I'm 20-years old, and I live near a small town in Wayne County, West Virginia, called Lavallette. My family and I originally lived in Jacksonville, Florida during my childhood, but we eventually moved up north because we couldn't handle the humidity and oncoming hurricanes. Now, what I am about to tell you guys is 100% true and I swear upon my life that what I've experienced is something I'll never forget.

It was last autumn on August 27, 2017, when my experiences first began. It was a Saturday evening between 6:30-7:30 p.m. I was on my way home from taking an incredibly long drive. I drove from my home to the town of Wayne, then past Tolsia and Louisa, and finally, as far as Chapmanville. I guess I drove way too far for my liking.

Anyway, it was getting dark, and I eventually found my way home in the form of a road called Eighth Street, near Lavallette, that led me to Mount Union Road. It was the road that took me straight to the house of one of my dad's friends, Ezra. That is where I got onto Walnut Gap Road that would take me home.

Now, on this road, there is a blind curve next to an old, abandoned white church. I always slow down before driving around the curve, just to make sure nobody is going to come flying around the corner. Right where I do that, there's a six-foot ledge on the left side of the road where some small trees have fallen over. On the other side, there's a steep hillside that has a path cleared through the thick underbrush where deer like to hide. And right at that same spot is where my first encounter happened.

Just as I slowly drove around the corner, I saw this… thing step onto the road on all fours. When I first saw it, I thought it was a 500-pound male black bear because it was the same size as one, and we do tend to have a few roaming around where I live now. But then, I noticed that it was more like a wolf because it had a long bushy tail, pointed ears, a canine-like snout, the same body shape as a wolf with jet-black hair and glowing, amber-colored eyes.

By the time it stepped onto the road, the wolf turned its head towards my direction and stared right at me. I was ecstatic at first to see a wolf in the wild, but at the same time, I realized there was something rather… off about my encounter. There should not be a wolf out there this big. In fact, the more I think about it, there shouldn't even be any wolves here in West Virginia anymore since the timber wolves that once lived in these woods were killed off.

Was the state government secretly using conservation efforts to repopulate wolves here in the state? Did a pack of wolves escape from a wildlife sanctuary and somehow found their way here? If so, then how did this one get so freaking huge? Not only did the wolf's abnormal size catch my attention, so did the look in its eyes. They looked different from what I see in the eyes of any canine I know of. They looked much more intelligent than anything I've ever seen.

Whatever theories I had to support any rational explanation for this unusual sighting were immediately shot away when this creature did something I'll never forget for the rest of my life. It was something that still haunts my soul to this very day. When we both stared at each other, even while I'm inside of my car, I heard what sounded like bones popping loudly. To my absolute shock, I watched this wolf place its hand on top of my car hood, raise itself off the ground, and stand up on two legs. Yeah, you heard me right, it wasn't

a paw it placed on my car hood, it was a hand. When the wolf stood up and my headlights hit it square-on, that's when I got a good look at it.

It was easily eight-feet tall and weighed 600-650 pounds or more. As I said, it was covered in jet-black hair that seemed quite feral, as if it hasn't been cleaning himself that much, and it also had a long, bushy tail and two glowing amber-yellow eyes. To my shock, it was more than a wolf standing on its hind legs. It had a human-like torso from the waist up that appeared muscular with broad shoulders and long forearms, longer than those of a normal human being. I could see the muscles of this "Wolfman" pulsating with each breath it took, especially in the headlights.

It also had these dexterous hands that looked almost like raccoon hands, but with more elongated fingers and long, jet-black claws at each fingertip. They looked like they could be used to easily manipulate any kind of prey in its clutches. They also looked like they could easily rip me to shreds, or maybe they can do more than just that. The hind legs resemble more like those of a dog or wolf. This I can easily tell because they bent backwards and had these massive paws for feet, and from the looks of which, it was standing on his toes more than on his feet.

It had a massive head like that of a wolf or a large German Shepard, but bigger in proportion. It also had pointed ears and tuffs of fur at the tip of each ear, as well as a long muzzle with these great, big fangs gouging out at the front of his snout. To be honest with you, the fangs had a very eerie resemblance to those of a Smilodon or saber-toothed cat, but the rest of it just looked like a werewolf.

But the eyes… the eyes were the one thing, the only thing about my encounter that night, that I'll never forget. Even writing about it to you all right now sends a bone-chilling fear down my spine. As I've said to you prior, the eyes looked extremely intelligent, far smarter than any animal I've ever come to know in my neck of the woods. But they also held a feeling that told me I was looking into the eyes of something that just spelled evil out of them.

Finally, I gained this overwhelming sense of dread after seeing it walk to my side of the car on two legs. It slowly bent down to level its eyes with mine, and I froze in pure, unadulterated horror when it used its hand to jiggle the door handle to try to open my car door. Fortunately, all the doors to my car were locked, and every window was closed, but this still horrified me to a point where I couldn't even breathe.

This Wolfman, as I previously referred to it as, gave out a grunt and frowned at me for a few seconds before standing back up and walking to the other side of my car. It jiggled the other door handle adjacent to the passenger side. Whatever this thing was, it was intelligent enough to know what a doorknob or, in this case, a door handle is for.

At this point, I was absolutely shaking in my driver's seat, with that same fear still latched onto my soul. Have you ever been through an experience in your life where, even though you have known all your life that you're an apex predator, you find yourself going out into the wilderness alone, and you suddenly feel so weak, so vulnerable, so helpless in the eyes of such a beast like this? That's exactly how I felt at the time of my encounter.

I felt like this thing, a creature that shouldn't even exist, yet it was standing right there in front of my car, was the true ruler of the forest and we humans were nothing compared to what it can really do. It could have easily ripped the doors off my car and pulled me out of it, it could've caught up to me if I tried to escape, and even if I tried to scream for help, it wasn't going to help me because I knew how powerful this predator was, even if I don't know it yet.

Just by looking at the "Wolfman," I knew a human being wouldn't have stood a chance against it, and I knew… that it knew that I knew. I honestly thought I was going to die that night and my family and friends would never

see me again. I thought that they would never know that I was about to be killed or eaten alive by something no one even believes existed, and that there was nothing I could do about it.

However, none of that ever happened to me. It was as if God were watching over me that night, protecting me from the malevolent beast that was circling me. Instead of attacking me head on, the Wolfman bared its teeth at me and let out an extremely deafening snarl. It then walked around the front side of my car and crossed the road on its hind legs in just two steps. The encounter didn't end there, though. By the time it crossed the road, it paused for a couple of seconds before it slowly turned around to look at me one last time.

As soon as it did that, I could've sworn right there and then that it wasn't alone. I looked over its shoulders and I could see multiple pairs of eyes staring directly at me. I knew they were the same creatures as the first one because they held the same eye-shine and gave off the same growls, too. I estimate that I saw at least five other pairs of eyes staring at me. Three of the pairs were low to the ground on all fours, the other two were standing upright... but they didn't reveal themselves out of the darkness like the first one did. In my opinion, I think he was the alpha male of this pack. If you all think encountering one werewolf-like creature was terrifying enough, imagine how I felt when I saw there was more than one creature there with this one.

With that scary thought, I snapped out of my trance and decided to get the hell out of there. Slamming hard on the accelerator, I bolted away and drove out of there like a bat out of hell. I'm not pulling your leg here, but the distance from right where I was when I saw those things to my home... I literally arrived home and pulled into the garage in just one minute.

By the time I arrived, I was in tears. I've never felt that scared before in my entire life, and not only that, but that was also the first time I've cried that much in a long time. My parents were concerned about the state I was in and asked me what happened. I basically told them everything that transpired just before I pulled in.

Now, I may have made up different stories and stuff before, but that was only when I was so little. Whatever I've experienced wasn't a joke. I told them the whole truth with honesty, but terror in my voice. But of course, they didn't believe me. They just assumed that what I saw could've been a black bear and driving after dark like that makes your mind play tricks on you, but this wasn't a trick I saw. I was 19 at the time, but I respected the DUI laws (Driving Under the Influence) so I wasn't drunk while driving home that night. I wasn't dreaming of this incident, nor was I hallucinating it. It wasn't even a simple misidentification. I know what I saw, and there's no doubt in my mind that it was real.

After this encounter, it affected me so much that I was forced to isolate myself from everyone I know, including my family and friends, for a little over a month or two. But I eventually broke out of my shell and got back into the social life again. However, I took this time to do some intense research on what I saw, and that's when I came upon the Dogman phenomenon for the first time.

According to several eyewitness testimonies, people have reported seeing the same exact creatures all over the United States and even in some remote parts of the world. This filled me with relief, knowing that I wasn't alone, that there are people out there who swear on their lives, and even to this day, that what they saw out there was real.

They're not a haunting part of humanity's imagination like we all believe them to be. Monsters do exist in this world, and this fact alone makes us realize how small our world really is. It makes me wonder that if a pack of werewolf-like creatures can exist, then what else could be out there lurking in the shadows, watching us with intelligent eyes, waiting for us to prove their existence in man's world?"

In December 2020, three girls were returning from Christmas shopping in West Virginia. As they made their way home, they were on an old Country Road near the Border of Kentucky, when it began to rain and turn rather foggy. They slowed down due to the low visibility and poor road conditions.

The road on which they traveled had open farmland on the right and heavy woods on the left. Out of nowhere, the group saw a very large animal come from their left out of the woods. It started to cross the road directly in front of their vehicle, causing the driver to hit the brakes, and come to a complete stop trying to avoid a collision with the beast.

At first glimpse, the women thought it was a large bear, which isn't that unusual in West Virginia. As the car headlights lit the creature up, they described its fur as being black with some tan tinge to it around the face and chest area. That's when the trio realized it wasn't a bear because the creature stood up on its hind legs, at approximately the halfway point, while crossing the road. It was at this time the monster turned its head, looking directly at them into the car.

The Driver described it as having a head like a wolf or a German Sheppard dog, it eyes glowed in the headlights, causing the girls to all scream out loud. One witness described it as being at least seven feet tall and three feet wide at the shoulders. The other girl said as the dog-like creature began to use its arms like a person, it snarled its teeth letting out a very loud growl while looking into the car.

The creature then went back down to all fours, continuing across the road, letting out another loud growl as it leapt over a 5-foot fence. It continued across the open field at an abnormally fast speed, reaching the far side of the field in a matter of just a few seconds, disappearing into the wood line on the far side of the field.

All three women wished to remain anonymous and to keep the exact location a secret for fear of too much publicity near their homes and family farms. But all three were very adamant that they knew this thing was 100% not a bear. All three were scared to death. When they returned home to share their stories with friends and family, they were told that it had to be a bear.

Near the end of winter in 2022 a man named J Spencer was traveling to work early in the morning. It was snowing lightly in the darkness just before dawn. He had traveled passed Sam Black Church on interstate I 64, and was near the first bridge, that is called a bridge to nowhere, or Paul Bunion's picnic table by locals. Just then, in the blink of an eye, an enormous canine like animal ran across I 64 from left to right, crossing in front of his Ford F150 pickup truck. Taken totally by surprise, Mr. Spencer had to take a minute or so to process what he had just seen. Once he had gathered himself, he realized that it was most definitely a wolf.

During my interview with Mr. Spencer, he said the back of the wolf was level with the hood of his truck. He described its body, without the tail, as being as long as the front of his truck. The creature was colored black on its back, and the rest that he could see was a gray and white. He was almost positive that his truck must have at least hit the tail of the beast, as it narrowly escaped certain death or injury by being hit by the moving truck.

Once he got to work, he called his friend who runs a John Deere dealership in Lewisburg, West Virginia. He asked his friend if he, or anyone else he knows, has ever seen unusually large dogs running amuck in the area. His friend responded by saying, do mean wolves? He said yes, wolves. His friend proceeded to tell him that yes, people are seeing these wolves regularly because they are coming down from Coal Knob to the sheep farms in Ashbury to feed.

It has long been known that wolves had been eradicated in West Virginia over a hundred years ago and it is fact that the Timberwolves in North America had been on the endangered species list years ago, but have recently made a comeback. It would make sense that the wolf could have easily migrated back into West Virginia, Canada and other parts of North America.

But what about the unusual size of this wolf during this encounter and others such as mine on Pals Mountain several years ago? Is this simply Timberwolves making a comeback and migrating into areas where the food and cover is beneficial to their survival, or is this something more ominous and darker going on here in the Mountain State? If you consider all the legends, sightings, and encounters being reported of giant wolves, dogmen, and werewolves, you might be left with more questions than answers. Let's not forget that hunters have been hunting these creatures for as long as they have been around. That makes me think that some of them, if not most, of the Dogmen or Werewolf type creatures being reported, are and can be considered evil in nature.

Chapter VIII

Recent

Modern Day Wolf Cults
and Paramilitary Units

One would think that wolf cults would be something that ancient peoples would have been involved in, but there are vast numbers of these cults that exist worldwide to this day. Some of these cults have been in existence for hundreds, if not thousands, of years. I will touch on some of them in this chapter because I feel it is important to give you, the reader, a sense of what is going on around you. These things may be in the dark shadows of alley-ways of any given city. They may be in your own neighborhood, in the dark woods and deep dark hollows in your local forest, for you never know what is lurking in the dark these days.

Most wolf cults were taken out during the vast witch hunts that were conducted in the 16th and 17th centuries by the church. Since those times, several have resurfaced and survived in other parts of the world. Some were founded in the 20th century, which saw a rise in spiritual and mystical thinking in the west. Other wolf cults have appeared with the growth of the new age and pagan groups over the last few decades.

One of the most well known and researched wolf cults is the lycaean Zeus Cult that stems from the remote southern mountain region of Greece in the Arcadia Mountain range. This group was said to believe in human sacrifice, and evidence of their existence dates to before Christ. The cult survived through the Turkish occupation of Greece and grew through the 1920s, when Nazi researchers investigated the area in the 1940s for signs of this elusive cult. It is known that the Axis powers during World War II were never able to completely conquer Arcadia.

Not to be confused with the Egyptian god Anubis, another Egyptian god named Wepwawet, who is known to be a god of war, had a cult that was thought to be extinct since ancient times. However, it is widely known that in the 1890s, the worship of this Deity was revived in France and Britain and that this cult group was run by intellectuals. It then spread into the military of both sides in World War I, and is especially used and practiced by special forces groups and assassins to this day.

Unlike other Werewolf cults, this group does not practice blood rituals or sacrifices, but only seeks the advancement of its members. It is said its members can shapeshift into wolf form and have other supernatural abilities that include the ability to move in complete silence, otherworldly speed and even the ability to be invisible.

In Norse mythology, there is a wolf called Fenrir. It is said to be one of pure evil, monstrous in size and will be the entity that kills Odin in the end of the world battle of Ragnarok.

There is a modern-day cult of Fenrir that dates to around 1933. Events that transpired in Germany inspired the growth of Nordic pride along with fascist politics across the land. Some of the more violent Neo Nazi group's adopted Fenrir even the SS Wiking Division worshiped him.

This cult was and is very violent, and you can bet that it still exists today in parts of the world. They practice ritual bloodletting, test of strength and fe-

rocity to name a few. Documents recovered by U.S. intelligence officers say that the SS Werewolf troops were members of this cult. At the end of the War the cult went underground, but modern reports say that it is alive and growing, especially among white supremacist groups around the world.

Today the cult consists of werewolf officers and human prospects. The human prospects are said to have to go through a series of tests and initiations before ever being considered for actual Lycanthropy. The cult does appear on law enforcement watch lists from around the world. Although considered too spread out and a bit unorganized, the cult is not considered to be high on the dangers list. However, concerned agencies feel that if a leader would happen to take over the group, it most definitely become a much more dangerous cult.

I first came across reports of Werewolf Paramilitary units while stationed in Italy in the mid-1990s. I was a member of NATO forces during the Bosnia-Kosovo War, and I am a veteran of that war. It makes sense that worship and cult activism of the werewolf cults that were adopted by military personnel over the years still exists today. The fact remains that they do still exist in various means around the world.

One such organization is called the brothers of Fenrir. This cult is Neo Nazi and has ties to biker gangs and organized crime. Founded in 2007, in Sweden, it has spread to Norway and Denmark. They are a particularly nasty bunch who have been known to attack foreign owned businesses and communities using intimidation tactics. Police agencies across these countries consider them volatile, very dangerous and growing in number.

Another group is known as the Hounds of God. This group is a secret society of Werewolves that is sworn to combat witches, witchcraft, and other supernatural threats. This group also participated in uprisings against the Nazis, and the Soviet Union. It is based out of Latvia and Lithuania, and dates to the 11th century.

A group based here in the United States, out of Idaho, who is called the Broken Mountain Republic, came onto the FBI's radar as a localized ecoterrorist group. They have been known to stage attacks on local and federal law enforcement facilities in the state. They claimed responsibility for the deaths of Idaho Department of Game and Fish officers during a local wolf cull in 2014. The local coroner says that their deaths were caused by large wolves. This I find striking, since members of this group claim to be werewolves. But nevertheless, it is quite compelling.

A group out of Ireland, called the Ossory Volunteers, are believed to be a splinter branch of the IRA. They have been linked to gun running, and even assassinations in Europe and North Africa. Intercepted communications from various spy agencies have confirmed that members of this group are working as mercenaries in locations around the world such as Ukraine, and Chechnya.

The Mures Brigade, who was active during the Transylvania ethnic events in the 1990s, is a Romanian Militia dedicated to ridding Hungarians from the country. It has many sympathizers in local and federal government, and is on the CIA's watch list due to some of its members having fought in Bosnia as volunteer mercenaries.

Chapter IX

Dogmen and ET's

Although there isn't much evidence to support this theory out there, some say that there is at least one race of extraterrestrial Dogman type of creature that have been visiting the Earth for thousands of years. As far as West Virginia goes, we all know the number of strange happenings that go on here. So, it is not a far stretch to say, that it could be possible, that some of these Dogmen sightings in the Mountain State, could quite possibly be alien in nature or even interdimensional.

The 'twenty and backers' are said to be members of specialized government military units that deal with extraterrestrials on other planets. According to some of these experiencers, the creatures are manufactured by a more advanced alien race known as the Draconians. They explain that they are part biological tissue and part machine. They claim to have fought them on numerous occasions on various planets, including here on Earth.

What is compelling to me is that the subjects being interviewed, were put through rigorous lie detector tests. All who were interviewed passed those tests on numerous occasions before they were ever allowed to tell their stories on various episodes of one television broadcast.

According to these experiencers and various sources, at some point the U.S. Air Force made a deal with an extraterrestrial race, known as the Nordics, to recruit personnel into their secret space program. In the deal, the Air Force could only recruit individuals for twenty years at a time. As part of the deal, they were given new technology in exchange for this. With this high-tech, they can age digress people and wipe their mind clean of any memories of having served in the 20 and back program. After these people had been mind wiped, and age regressed, they are sent back via a portal to where they started when they were abducted. In doing this, it is believed that these ET's can somehow manipulate timelines.

Some have said that top Air Force brass and the military industrial complex had been planning and developing this program for many years. However, it wasn't implemented until after the solar warden program was activated in 1984.

This program was initially reserved to military personnel only, but it was soon realized the program needed civilians to be involved as well. Having said that, it is thought that a very small percentage of civilians are a part of the program. The civilians that are used, only do small tours like 4 months to 18 months instead of years, even though some involved have stated they did the entire 20 years tour. It is said that 20 and backs that are only allowed to do a maximum of three tours due to the danger of participants suffering mental issues with any more tours than that.

Here on earth, we know about the ancient Egyptian God called Anubis, which has the head of a Jackal and the body of a man, very similar to more modern werewolf descriptions. Many out there feel that these ancient gods were in fact extraterrestrials. Those who subscribe to the ancient astronaut theory, believe many of the ancient gods such as Anubis, Horace and many others from different cultures, such as Zeus in Greek Mythology and even Jesus Christ, were, in fact, extraterrestrial in origin.

As an investigator, we must look at these claims from outside the box to give ourselves a broader prospective of the possibilities of these theories having any truth to them. Frequently these "Gods" were described to have had abilities to bring people and animals back from the dead, heal people that were dying with a simple touch or wave of their hand or the slightest touch. Some were said to carry special objects that gave them unbelievable powers that would say allow them to move giant blocks of stone weighing hundreds of tons with relative ease. Still yet these special staffs, or wand like objects, could knock things out of the sky by simply pointing it at them. As investigators, we must ask ourselves, were these weapons or wands divinely inspired tools or instruments, or were they really a much more advanced technology from a superior race of beings.

Whatever you feel about these claims, you cannot ignore the facts that these types of beings, as well as stories of miraculous events, have been talked about for thousands of years by many different races with varying cultural backgrounds and belief systems. These stories often have way more similarities than differences, which leads one to believe that there is or may be some truth to these beings once inhabiting the earth and even other planets in the universe.

In the late 1960s, there was a massive wave of UFO sightings in the United States, especially in the Ohio River Valley. From these sightings spawned a great variety of strange cases, including the Mothman Phenomena.

One of these cases was the curios case of a man named Tad Jones. Mr. Jones was from a suburb of Charleston known as Dunbar, West Virginia. I covered this account in the *Real West Virginia UFO Sightings and Encounters* book. As I have said for many years, some of these sightings and encounters often interconnected in some way, shape or form. For example, a UFO sighting may not only be a sighting of a strange unidentified craft in the sky, it could also be an encounter with a strange being or creature in some cases. That makes it a dual threat, depending on what kind of creature was seen or encountered. Or perhaps some evidence was found at the scene, that doesn't quite match up, nor does it make any sense in relation to the sort of evidence one might expect to find in the case of a UFO sighting.

In Mr. Jones case, this seems to be one of those instances. He was known as a God-fearing man and not one to partake in the consumption of drink or

drugs. He was hardworking and had an honest reputation. Early one morning in January 1966, Jones was on his way to work at the store he managed. Little did he know his usual drive was about to lead him into a whole new world of the strange and unexplained that, still to this day, have yet to be solved.

While driving his route to work, at approximately 9 a.m., on I 64, he observed what he thought was a road work crew. However, as he drew closer, he realized it was not that at all. He would soon discover something out of this world. He saw a large spherical shaped craft hovering just several feet above the roadway. It had a dull aluminum luster to it and was reported as being roughly twenty feet in circumference. It sported two antennae, four legs and some sort of propeller like apparatus on the ship. Furthermore, it had some sort of wheels on the bottom of the legs, and it had a small window, only about nine inches round in size, on the side that faced him. He said that when he first drove up on it, that it appeared to be in some sort of idling mode. As he continued observing the strange machine, it began to spin faster and faster, rising upward at the same time, and that he watched it disappear out of sight in the sky.

His sighting left him in shambles, and he spent some time contemplating what he had seen. He decided to contact the police and report the entire ordeal. After that, it didn't take long for his experience to be featured all over the local papers. Around the same time, he woke up one morning and discovered a piece of paper had been slipped under his door. To his dismay, the note read, "We know what you have seen, and we know that you have talked. You better keep your mouth shut." It was a very disturbing to say the least, and Mr. Jones had no idea of who could have written such a note nor where it could have come from. Jones became paranoid and was constantly watching out for people following him.

A local man named Ralph Jarrett, who was considered by some to be the local expert on such matters, soon became aware of Tad's sighting and was eager to learn more, especially since he had some strange experiences himself. It wasn't long before Jarrett reached out to Jones and during their meeting, he uncovered many never heard details of the sighting. He discovered that the UFO had been hovering over a major gas line. As Jarrett continued with his investigation, Jones once again received a threatening note slipped under his door. This note was on a torn piece of cardboard with burnt edges and stated simply, "There won't be another warning." The intensity was ramping up during this investigation and soon garnered the attention of John Keel, who was already in the area investigating the massive UFO wave that was being reported in the Ohio River Valley.

While Keel was interviewing Jones, he mentioned to him that one week after his sighting, while driving the same route, he noticed a man by himself along the roadside. He pulled over and asked him if he needed help, but got no response whatsoever except for a wave. The next day the man was in the same spot of the road. Jones conveyed to Keel that he got an overwhelming sense that there was something off with the man, and the whole encounter was very unsettling.

He described the man as being very tan and appeared to be wearing some sort of blue uniform. He was carrying, what looked like some sort of instrument, in a box, with a large dial on it, like a clock with wiring coming from it and going to his other hand. Jones claimed he now felt that it was tied somehow to his sighting. Here's where the whole account gets weirder, as Keel is investigating all of this and trying to find any rational explanations to it all, he decides to go out to the site of Jones experience. Keel found a strange series of footprints that appeared to be from an enormous dog of some type. In his estimation, the dog would have to have weighed at least two hundred pounds. In addition to the dog tracks, he found among them, an unusual human track and some other anomalies. His description is as follows in his report.

"As well as the dog tracks, we found a single footprint of what seemed to be a large naked human foot. This track was in the mud, with no other footprints of any kind around it. Casts were made of these tracks and sent off to be analyzed, they were not able to be identified as any known animal in the area."

Keel claimed that the famous cryptozoologist Ivan Sanderson told him that similar dog tracks often appeared in locations that displayed a high level of paranormal activity. He went on to say that he later encountered tracks like these around the country in separate cases. So, it would seem, even in Mr. Jones' case, that they were all left with more questions than answers.

My whole point in sharing this case, in this chapter, is merely to show that reports of giant unknown dog tracks have been found on numerous occasions, around the country for many years in areas that UFOs have been sighted and where other anomalous activities have occurred. I'm not saying that these dog men are definitely of extraterrestrial nature. But this is very interesting, and makes for a good lead regarding the question of is there a race of dogmen that could be of extraterrestrial origin. For me, it is very exciting and tantalizing to discover these little tidbits of information. As researchers and investigators, all we can do is keep collecting and accounts of experiences and gathering any evidence that is found along the way.

Conclusion

When it comes to Dogmen and Werewolves, there is simply no scientific evidence known to exist that proves these creatures are walking among us. That is, barring any secret information, that is only known to a small number of military or scientific entities. What there is, however, is a plethora of circumstantial evidence indicating that there is not just one thing people are seeing, or encountering, around the world and in West Virginia. I believe there are several types of animals, as well as beings, being seen and encountered not only here in W.V. but also around the world. The eyewitness descriptions of these animals or beings are very similar at times, but at other times they vary enough to assume that there are several different creatures being encountered. The fact remains that there are countless trustworthy and credible people out there claiming to have had some sort of encounter with a Dogman or Werewolf type of being.

After you have read some of the historical accounts in this book along with some of the claims of the '20 and backers,' some of it seems to match up. If one shred of their claims is true, then it is an eye-opening conclusion to say the least. No matter how you look at it, the dogman enigma it is truly fascinating to say the least and quite unnerving as well.

These creatures have been talked about and documented in historical writings, paintings, drawings, and carvings for thousands of years by various cultures around the world. This historical evidence comes from varying time periods, on multiple continents, and was created by different people who never had contact with one another. That makes for a compelling argument in and of itself. Could it be that much of our history has been hidden from us? Could it be that the governments of the world have somehow conspired against us to keep the truth hidden away in some locked vault under the Vatican or in some secret government storage locker? One can only guess.

Whether it's an ancient curse, a punishment on an old bloodline for a crime committed, or even an extraterrestrial race still surviving in small numbers on earth, one thing is certain, sightings and encounters with these beasts will definitely continue throughout our world, and here in West Virginia. You can mark my words, I will continue to investigate and research these encounters for as long as I am able, with the hope that I can contribute something, legitimate enough, to make the case for their existence.

Until then, all we can do as investigators is to continue to interview, document and investigate the mysterious cases of the Dogman.

About the Author

Dave Spinks

After having a terrifying encounter with a Bigfoot with his paternal grandfather and a few years later experiencing an after-death visit from his maternal grandfather, Dave Spinks became fascinated by the paranormal and started his search for answers. Gathering evidence in the form of EVP's, video and photographic data and personal experiences, Dave collected experiences from many different people from all walks of life including law enforcement officers, farmers, hunters, schoolteachers, doctors and more. Dave cites *In Search Of,* with Leonard Nimoy and Hans Holzer as a few of his many early influences.

As an adult, he joined the USAF right out of college and became a trained observer. He spent eight years active duty and one in the Army National Guard.

After the military, Dave pursued a career in law enforcement, working for the West Virginia Department of Corrections for two years and moving into federal law enforcement with the U.S. Department of Justice for another eight years.

His professional path greatly enhanced his investigative skills. During his years working in the federal and state government, he continued his pursuit of the supernatural, investigating and researching anytime he had an opportunity.

His service in the military gave him the opportunity to investigate locations in Italy while stationed there in the 1990s.

In 2011, he retired from law enforcement and decided to dive headlong into the pursuit of the paranormal on a full-time basis.

Since that time, he has worked alongside some of the most well-known names in the various fields of the paranormal including John Zaffis, Rosemary Ellen Guiley, Dr. Ray Keller, Eric Altman, and many more

In 2017 Dave purchased the notorious haunted location known as Willows Weep in Cayuga, Indiana. The sole purpose in him doing so was to have a paranormal lab in which to attempt to document and study paranormal phenomena as it occurs. Look for more on this location in the future.

Dave has investigated, researched, and written about a variety of topics including cryptids, hauntings and Ufology.

He has been a featured speaker at numerous conferences around the country, and is often asked to lecture on a variety of paranormal topics.

He has been a featured guest on countless radio shows and paranormal podcasts from around the world including *Coast to Coast Am*, *Spaced Out Radio*, *Arcane Radio*, and other radio programs. Dave has appeared on several network television shows including *Destination America's, Terror in the Woods. The Travel Channel's, Ghost Nation, These Woods are Haunted, Paranormal 911*, and *In Search of Monsters* as well as the *History Channel's UnXplained* season 1 and 2, as well as *Discovery Channel's Expedition X*. In

Author Dave Spinks filming on location.

2018 he was featured in the *Small Town Monsters* movie, *The Flatwoods Monster, 'A legacy of Fear.'* And the movie *Flatwoods*.

Dave has also co-produced several Investigation videos on DVD including: *Willows Weep, Malefice, Fonti Flora, Point Pleasant Files* Vol 1, *Haunting of Sweet Springs, Ghost of the Guyer Opera House, 1699, A Haunting in Bellaire* and *House of Haunted Fields*. He is constantly conducting investigations, adding to his knowledge and experiences.

Dave's books include: *West Virginia Bigfoot, Real West Virginia Hauntings* Series Vol 1, 2 and 3, *Real West Virginia UFO's, Willows Weep, Wicked 46*, and *Cooking with Cryptids*. He has also contributed to the wildly popular *Wood Knocks* Series by David Weatherly. Dave has several new works in progress, so be on the lookout for those as well.

"I love to share what I do with others, in the hopes of answering some of man's greatest questions: Is there life after death? Are there unknown creatures walking among us? Are we alone in the universe? I believe there is something after death. We are not alone, and that there are unknown creatures walking among us. Finding answers is my motivation."

TO FIND DAVE ONLINE
http://www.davespinksparanormalinvestigator.com
https://www.facebook.comdsworldofweird/
https://www.facebook.com/DaveSpinksRealSupernatural/ADDITIONAL
INFORMATION

Dave Spinks World of Weird

This is your one-stop shop in West Virginia for all things paranormal and supernatural. You can buy all sorts of merch here. You can even get paranormal equipment, take a haunted walking tour, or go on a Bigfoot hunt. Report an experience or sighting to Dave, or one of his team members, for further investigation. There are book signings, paranormal conferences, classes, a holistic healing center, psychic readings and more right at the store. There is no other place like it.

Open Wednesday through Saturday, 1 p.m. to 7 p.m. Check Facebook for holidays and possible changes in hours of business.

43 Oakford Ave
Richwood W.V.
Visit dsworldofweird on Facebook
1-304-619-4155

Ken Gerhard

Ken Gerhard is a widely recognized cryptozoologist and field investigator for The Centre for Fortean Zoology, as well as a fellow of the Pangea Institute and consultant for several research organizations. He has traveled the world searching for evidence of mysterious animals and legendary beasts including Bigfoot, the Loch Ness Monster, the Chupacabra, enigmatic winged creatures and werewolves.

In addition to co-hosting the *History Channel* TV series *Missing in Alaska*, Ken has appeared in three episodes of the television series *Monster Quest* and is featured in the *History Channel* special *The Real Wolfman*, as well as other series including: *Ancient Aliens* (*History Channel*), *True Monsters* (*History Channel*), *Unexplained Files* (*Science Channel*), *Legend Hunters* (*Travel Channel*), *Paranatural* (*National Geographic*), *Weird or What?* *with William Shatner* (*Syfy*), *Monsters and Mysteries in America* (*Animal Planet*), *True Supernatural* (*Destination America*),*Ultimate Encounters* (*TruTV*), *Monster Project* (*Nat Geo Wild*) and *Shipping Wars* (*A&E*).

His credits include appearances on numerous news broadcasts and radio programs like *Coast-to-Coast AM*, as well as being featured in articles by the *Associated Press*, *Houston Chronicle* and *Tampa Tribune*.

Ken is an author which has contributed to trade publications including *Fate Magazine*. He currently lectures and exhibits at various conferences and events across the United States.

Born on Friday the 13th of October 1967 (exactly one week before the famous Patterson Bigfoot footage was shot), Ken has traveled to twenty-six different countries on six continents and has visited virtually each of the United States. An avid adventurer, he has camped along the Amazon, explored the Galápagos, hiked the Australian Outback and has visited many ancient and mysterious sites, from Machu Pichu to Stonehenge.

Visit

http://www.kengerhard.com/

Cosmic Ray
Raymond A. Keller, Ph.D
Headline Books

Dr. Raymond A. Keller, II, a retired history professor currently serving as an Ameri-Corps VISTA at In Touch and Concerned, a United Way agency providing accessible and affordable transportation options for persons with disabilities, seniors and veterans in Monongalia County, West Virginia, has recently come out with his second book, *Venus Rising: A Concise History of the Second Planet*, 336 pages, illustrated. Dr. Keller's book explores many facets of conditions and life on Venus in many dimensions from a perspective of conspiracies, history, theosophy, ufology and current events, especially space research. To date, *Venus Rising* has won wild card awards at both the Southern California and London, United Kingdom, book festivals. Dr. Leo Sprinkle of the University of Wyoming at Laramie and Hakan Blomqvist of the UFO Archives in Sweden, wrote the introductions; and Michael LaRiche of the *Northeast Ohio Coast-to-Coast A.M. Radio Discussion Groups* wrote the foreword for Dr. Keller's book. Dr. Keller has lived and worked in 44 different countries and has been writing about UFOs and paranormal activity since 1967. He was the founder and director of the Outer Space International

Research and Investigations Society of Hilmar, California, as well as the publisher and co-editor of the *New Millennial Star*, a monthly pre-internet tabloid newspaper with a circulation of 7,500 copies. He received his doctoral degree from West Virginia University in 2011, focusing on various aspects of the African and Basque settlement of Venezuela; and he received his master's degree from the same institution in 2004, majoring in foreign language, with an emphasis on magic realism in Latin American literature. Married to Ydalis M. Herrera of Venezuela, they reside in Morgantown, West Virginia.

Ron Lanham
Artist, Paranormal Investigator, Host of Wild & Weird Radio

Ron has a background in art, both physical and 3D, as well as music and video and has worked to produce 3D content for various multimedia projects. The most recent was producing art for the book *Cooking with Cryptids* by Dave Spinks. He has been involved in paranormal and UFO research for over thirty years. Following a personal experience at an early age, he became interested in paranormal phenomena which led to founding his first research project, Ghost Watch RIP, over a decade ago. Later, Ron founded Wild & Weird West Virginia ,with friend and business partner Joe Perdue and is also a host of the *Wild & Weird Radio Podcast*. Ron has been asked to speak at several events and was featured in the *Small-Town Monsters* films *The Mothman Legacy* and *On the Trail of UFOs, Dark Sky*. Ron's most recent project has been his work on the West Virginia High Strangeness Collective, a new community research project of Wild & Weird WV.

www.facebook.com/wildnweirdradio/
www.wildandweirdwv.com
Instagram @lanhamron
Wild & Weird WV linktree
https://linktr.ee/wildandweirdwv

Joedy Cook

Joedy Cook is a retired U.S. Army and Iraq war Veteran.

He is one of the most active Dogman & Bigfoot researchers in the state of Ohio. Originally, he was a member of the Cincinnati UFO research group A.S.K. but realized that his interests were more in the field of cryptozoology.

Joedy has been studying the Dogman and Bigfoot phenomenon since 1991 and is the author of several books. He founded the North America Dogman Project, Cryptid Seekers, as well as the Ohio Center for Bigfoot Studies.

He is co-producer of the *NADP* DVD Documentaries: *Wisconsin Werewolf, The Germantown Werewolf* and *The Beast of Land Between the Lakes.* Joedy has appeared on several television programs, which discuss large primates in North America, including the *History Channel's Monster Quest, Syfy Channel's Sightings & Encounters, The Learning Channel's Top Ten Mysteries of the World,* and *Destination America's Mysteries and Monsters in America Today.*

Joedy lives in Cincinnati and can be seen giving presentations at paranormal and cryptid conventions across the state and in Canada.

Look for these other titles available from

Unapologetically Authentic

by Jennifer L. Schwartz-Flack M.Ed, LPC, RMT

Willows Weep - by Dave Spinks

Cooking With Crytptids - Dave Spinks

Real West Virginia UFOs - Dave Spinks

A View From Appalachia, Seven Decades of Reflection

by Stanton Nolan Spinks

Coming Soon

CPR For the Soul

by Jennifer L. Schwartz-Flack M.Ed, LPC, RMT

The Monongahela Monster by Dave Spinks

Made in the USA
Middletown, DE
20 November 2025

22240829R00070